DATE DUE

APR 2 6 1994	
JUN 1 3 1994	
FEB 1 7 1996	
APR - 4 1996	
FEB 3 1998	
FEB 2 4 1998	
FEB 1 2 1999	
NOV - 7 2001	

BRODART   Cat. No. 23-221

CARING FOR CHILDREN IN LOW-INCOME FAMILIES

A Substudy of the National Child Care Survey, 1990

A NATIONAL ASSOCIATION FOR THE EDUCATION OF YOUNG CHILDREN (NAEYC) STUDY

Conducted by The Urban Institute

April A. Brayfield, Sharon Gennis Deich, and Sandra L. Hofferth

Sponsored by:

Administration for Children, Youth and Families, Office of Human Development Services, U.S. Department of Health and Human Services and The National Association for the Education of Young Children

URBAN INSTITUTE REPORT 93–2

THE URBAN INSTITUTE PRESS
Washington, D.C.

THE URBAN INSTITUTE PRESS
2100 M Street, N.W.
Washington, D.C. 20037

Library of Congress Cataloging in Publication Data

Caring for Children in Low-Income Families: A Substudy of the National Child Care Survey, 1990 / April A. Brayfield, Sharon Gennis Deich, and Sandra L. Hofferth

1. Child care services—United States. 2. Poor children—United States. I. Deich, Sharon Gennis. II. Hofferth, Sandra L. III. Title. IV. Series

HQ778.7.U6B73	1993	93-16112
362.7'08'6942—dc20		CIP

(Urban Institute Report; 93-2; ISSN 0897-7399)

ISBN 0-87766-586-9
ISBN 0-87766-587-7 (paperback)

Printed in the United States of America.

Distributed by University Press of America

4720 Boston Way	3 Henrietta Street
Lanham, MD 20706	London WC2E 8LU
	ENGLAND

URBAN INSTITUTE REPORTS are designed to provide rapid dissemination of research and policy findings. Each report contains timely information and is rigorously reviewed to uphold the highest standards of policy research and analysis.

The Urban Institute is a nonprofit policy research and educational organization established in Washington, D.C. in 1968. Its staff investigates the social and economic problems confronting the nation and government policies and programs designed to alleviate them. The Institute disseminates significant findings of its research through the publications program of its Press. The goals of the Institute are to sharpen thinking about societal problems and efforts to solve them, improve government decisions and performance, and increase citizen awareness of important policy choices.

Through work that ranges from broad conceptual studies to administrative and technical assistance, Institute researchers contribute to the stock of knowledge available to guide decision making in the public interest.

Conclusions or opinions expressed in Institute publications are those of the authors and do not necessarily reflect the views of staff members, officers or trustees of the Institute, advisory groups, or any organizations that provide financial support to the Institute.

Child Care Project Advisory Group

Douglas Besharov, American Enterprise Institute

Virginia Cain, National Institute of Child Health and Human Development

Elizabeth Farquhar, U.S. Department of Education

Victoria Fu, Department of Family and Child Development, Virginia Polytechnic and State University

Ellen Galinsky, Families and Work Institute

Frederic Glantz, Abt Associates

Robert Granger, Manpower Demonstration Research Corp.

Jeanne Griffith, National Center for Education Statistics, Department of Education

Cheryl Hayes, National Commission on Children

Helena Hicks, Department of Health and Human Resources, State of Maryland

Beverly Jackson, National Black Child Development Institute

Sheila Kamerman, Columbia University School of Social Work

Ellen Kisker, Mathematica Policy Research

Joann Kuchak, Macro Systems

Joan Lombardi, Early Childhood Specialist

Mark Menchik, U.S. Office of Management and Budget

Frank Mott, Ohio State University, Center for Human Resource Research

Martin O'Connell, U.S. Bureau of the Census

Ann O'Keefe, U.S. Department of the Navy

Deborah Phillips, Department of Psychology, University of Virginia

Harriet Presser, Department of Sociology, University of Maryland

Philip K. Robins, Department of Economics, University of Miami

Nicholas Zill, Child Trends

Merrily Beryreuther, U.S. Department of Health and Human Services (DHHS)

Larry Guerrero, DHHS

Marlys Gustafson, DHHS

Patricia Hawkins, DHHS

Sharon McGroder, DHHS

William Prosser, DHHS

Ann Segal, DHHS

J.D. Andrews, National Association for the Education of Young Children (NAEYC)

Marilyn Smith, NAEYC

Barbara Willer, NAEYC

Acknowledgments

Funding for this report was provided by the Assistant Secretary for Planning and Evaluation (ASPE) of the U.S. Department of Health and Human Services (DHHS). We gratefully acknowledge Sharon McGroder at ASPE for her guidance and support as the Project Officer for this substudy.

We also thank Patricia Divine-Hawkins at the Administration on Children, Youth and Families (DHHS) and Barbara Willer at the National Association for the Education of Young Children—the Project Officers for the National Child Care Survey 1990—and Ann Segal at ASPE for their helpful comments on various drafts of this report. We also thank Edward Bryant at Westat and Michael Battaglia at Abt Associates for developing the sampling plans and providing statistical advice, and Abt Associates for collecting the data. Pamela Holcomb, Research Associate at The Urban Institute, provided comments on earlier drafts of this report. We acknowledge research assistants Jennifer Berdahl and Michael Tilkin and computer programmers KaLing Chan and Thy Dao, who helped design the original computer programs for the main survey. Special appreciation goes to Jennifer Pack for preparing the figures and tables in this report. Finally, we thank the 973 low-income families who responded to the survey.

Abstract

This report examines the care arrangements of children under age 13 who are in families with annual incomes below $15,000, using nationally representative data from the National Child Care Survey 1990 and its low-income supplement.

Although many low-income children are cared for exclusively by their parents, supplemental care arrangements play an important part in the lives of the majority of low-income children. For many families, child care consists of a combination of arrangements--parents, relatives, nonrelatives, centers, and extracurricular activities; many children use more than one supplemental arrangment each week. One of the most important findings is that the care arrangements used by children with employed mothers are quite similar to those used by children with nonemployed mothers enrolled in education or training programs.

Child care financially burdens many families. Although low-income families are less likely to pay for child care and spend fewer dollars on care than high-income families, they spend a substantially greater share of their income on the care of their children. Families in poverty spend an even higher proportion of their family budget on child care than other low-income families. Nonetheless, the majority of low-income families report that they do not receive any financial assistance with their supplemental arrangements.

Contents

Figures

Executive Summary

This report examines the care arrangements of children under age 13 who are in families with annual incomes below $15,000. Findings are based on data from the National Child Care Survey 1990 and its low-income supplement. This study represents approximately 6.6 million low-income households with children under age 13 and the 12 million children under age 13 in these families. Three fundamental issues are investigated: (1) how low-income children are regularly cared for; (2) how much low-income families spend on child care; and (3) the preferences of low-income parents in caring for their children. The major highlights of this analysis are as follows:

- Although many low-income children are cared for exclusively by their parents, 65 percent of children under age 13 are in nonschool, supplemental care for some period of time on a regular weekly basis.

- Low-income children of single mothers are less likely than low-income children in two-parent families to be cared for solely by a parent.

- Low-income children under age 5 spend more time in nonschool, supplemental care than low-income children aged 5 to 12.

- The child care arrangements used by employed mothers and nonemployed mothers enrolled in education or training programs are quite similar. Low-income parents manage the child care demands of education and training programs in the same way as the child care demands of employment.

- The distribution of low-income children across different types of child care arrangements used for the greatest amount of time each week does not vary by poverty status or participation in the Aid to Families with Dependent Children (AFDC) program.

- Grandparents play a significant role in caring for low-income children, especially for children of single mothers and children in two-parent families where both parents are employed. Twenty-nine percent of children under age 5 and 20 percent of children aged 5 to 12 are cared for by their grandparents on a regular basis.

- Twenty percent of low-income children under age 5 and 10 percent of low-income children aged 5 to 12 are in a center-based program for some period of time on a regular weekly basis.

- Only a small proportion of low-income children care for themselves or are cared for by nonrelatives in the child's own home.

- Thirty percent of school-age children in low-income families take lessons or participate in sports or club activities on a regular basis.

- Twenty-nine percent of 4-year-olds living in poverty are enrolled in a Head Start program.

- Children of full-time employed mothers are more likely than children of part-time employed mothers to be in multiple supplemental care arrangements. A significant proportion of children of single mothers who are *not* employed use more than one supplemental arrangement on a regular basis.

- Among low-income families using supplemental care, 39 percent of those with a child under age 5 pay for the care of their youngest child; 36 percent of those with a child aged 5 to 12 pay for that care.

- About a quarter of employed mothers in low-income families pay for relative care.

- The majority of low-income families report that they do not receive any financial assistance with their supplemental care arrangements. Most low-income parents receiving assistance get help from the government; employers play only a minor role in helping low-income parents with their child care expenses.

- Although families in poverty are less likely to pay for care and spend fewer dollars on child care than other low-income families, they spend a substantially greater share of their income on the care of their children. For example, families in poverty with a child under age 5 spend an average of 27 percent of their family income on child care, whereas low-income families above 125 percent of the poverty line spend an average of 16 percent.

- Low-income parents relying on some form of supplemental care and low-income parents caring exclusively for their children report that they are equally satisfied with their current child care arrangements.

- Although almost all low-income parents report that they are satisfied with their child care arrangements, a significant proportion want to change the current arrangement or combination of arrangements for their youngest child.

- The majority of low-income parents who want to change child care arrangements prefer center-based programs. Low-income families currently relying on relatives as the main arrangement for their youngest child under age 5 are those most likely to want to change arrangements. Single mothers are more likely than two-parent families to want an alternative arrangement.

- Quality, not cost, is the reason cited most often by low-income parents who prefer an alternative arrangement.

Chapter One

Introduction

Although considerable information is available on the child care use of American families as a whole, little data exist on the child care use, expenditures, and preferences of low-income families. Even in large surveys by the U.S. Bureau of the Census, often there are too few low-income families, particularly welfare mothers, to analyze (see, for example, Brush 1987). To address these issues with nationally representative data for the first time, the Office of the Assistant Secretary for Planning and Evaluation (ASPE) of the U.S. Department of Health and Human Services (DHHS) provided funds for a low-income supplement (Low-Income Study) to the National Child Care Survey, 1990 (NCCS). Consequently, this report examines: (1) how low-income children are regularly cared for; (2) how much low-income families spend on child care; and (3) what kind of arrangements low-income parents prefer. We focus on differences among low-income families according to selected key characteristics of the household.

The National Child Care Survey, 1990, together with its several substudies, was designed to provide nationally representative data on child care supply and demand in the United States. In addition to the Low-Income Study, the main survey and substudy reports include:

❑ *The National Child Care Survey, 1990* (Hofferth et al. 1991), a nationally representative survey of U.S. households with children under age 13. This survey was jointly sponsored by the National Association for the Education of Young Children (NAEYC) and the Administration on Children, Youth, and Families (ACYF) of the U.S. Department of Health and Human Services.

❑ *The National Child Care Survey, 1990: Military Substudy,* a study of Navy and Marine Corps families in six sites and military families representing all four services in Honolulu County. Through an interagency agreement with the DHHS, the U.S. Department of the Navy (DON) provided funds for this separate survey of military families.

❑ *Family Day Care in the United States, 1990,* a study of individuals who provide child care in their homes. Through an interagency agreement with the DHHS, the U.S. Department of Education (DOE) provided funds for this study.

The research for these studies was conducted by The Urban Institute, based upon data collected in a telephone survey designed by The Urban Institute and conducted by Abt Associates in early 1990.

The NCCS was part of a larger research agenda designed to develop a comprehensive and accurate picture of the child care market. The U.S. Department of Education was another partner in this broader research. The Profile of Child Care Settings Study (PCS), a nationally representative study of licensed family day care homes and child care centers, was conducted in 1989–90 by Mathematica Policy Research (MPR) under contract to the DOE. Not only did the NCCS use the same questionnaires as the PCS for interviewing screened and linked providers, but the sampling plans for both the consumer and PCS samples were designed to collect data within the same geographic areas during the same time period. Together, the PCS and the NCCS provide an extensive look at child care supply and demand in the United States.[1]

Research Design and Sample

Because the main NCCS survey did not oversample low-income households, it could not by itself provide enough low-income families for separate analysis. Consequently, the Low-Income Study was designed to supplement the data that were obtained from the main survey with additional low-income households. Low-income households, defined as those with a total annual household income below $15,000 and at least one child under age 13, represent one-fifth of American families. Telephone prefix areas with a median household income below $15,000 located in the same counties as the main survey served as the sampling frame. A separate sample of low-income households was generated in these areas using random-digit-dialing (RDD) procedures.

A total of 430 interviews with eligible households were completed for the low-income supplement. The interview completion rate among eligible low-income households was 77.5 percent; the overall response rate was 58.4 percent. When these 430 completed consumer interviews were combined with the 672 low-income households from the main survey, a total of 1,102 households, interviewed between October 1989 and June 1990, were obtained. Unfortunately, some respondents misunderstood the screener's question— hearing $50,000 instead of $15,000. Thus, after data cleaning,

973 families with a total of 1,751 children under age 13 met the income eligibility requirements for the Low-Income Study.

Appendix A details the design effects and the degree of precision of the survey percentages.

Evaluation of Quality of Data for Low-Income Families

Some questions arose about the quality of the data on low-income families, particularly those on children enrolled in Head Start and their families. Consequently, Urban Institute staff checked the data to ensure that they were representative of the low-income population of the United States. As a result of these data checks, we are fully confident that within the margin of error due to sampling, our results do represent low-income families. Poor children, however, appear to be underestimated in our data. The reader should therefore be cautious about drawing conclusions based upon the sample of children. For more information on data quality, see appendix D.

———————

Note, chapter 1

1. For information on how to obtain data from the NCCS and the PCS, contact Dr. J.J. Card, Sociometrics Corporation, 170 State Street, Suite 260, Los Altos, CA 94022.

Chapter Two

A Profile of Low-Income Families in the United States

This study reports on the characteristics of 6.6 million low-income households with children under age 13 and the 12 million children under age 13 in these households. Although all these households and children share one characteristic in common—annual household incomes below $15,000—they differ as to ages of children, household structure and size, parental employment status, race/ethnicity, household income, poverty status, and whether or not they receive Aid to Families with Dependent Children (AFDC). Because of the diversity of low-income households and their children, we describe their child care arrangements, expenditures, and preferences according to key characteristics of the child and the family. This chapter profiles these key characteristics of low-income households and their children.

Age of Child

Table 2.1 presents population estimates for low-income households and children by detailed age groupings. In 1990, 56 percent of low-income households with children under age 13 had at least one preschool-age child (i.e., a child under age 5), totaling 3.7 million U.S. households and 4.9 million preschool-age children. An additional 2.9 million low-income households had a youngest child aged 5 to 12, representing over 7 million low-income children in that age group.

Household Type

Table 2.2 presents the distribution of household types by age of youngest child. In 1990, about 35 percent of all low-income households with children under age 13 were two-parent families. Twenty-six percent of two-parent families were dual-employed households, 55 percent had just one employed parent, and in 19 percent of these families neither parent worked for wages (not shown). Nevertheless, 9 percent of *all* low-income households with children under age 13 were dual-employed households. For these families, two incomes were not enough to raise their total family income to $15,000 per year.

Nearly 58 percent of all low-income households with children under age 13 were headed by single mothers in 1990 (table 2.2). Forty-five percent of these mothers were employed, representing 1.7 million low-income mothers with children under age 13. Another 2.1 million low-income single mothers, of which 1.3 million had a child under age 5, were not working for wages in 1990.

Only a small proportion (less than 2 percent) of low-income households with children under age 13 were headed by single fathers in 1990 (table 2.2). And, finally, in 5 percent of low-income households with children requiring care (about

TABLE 2.1

Distribution of Low-Income Households and Children, by Age of Child

Households with Children Under Age 13	
Age of Youngest Child	Households (%)
Under 1	14.9
1–2	25.2
3–4	16.1
5	7.9
6–9	24.1
10–12	11.9
Under 5	56.1
5–12	43.9
Total	100.0
Sample size[a]	973
Population estimate (in thousands)	6,653
Children Under Age 13	
Age of Child	Children (%)
Under 1	8.6
1–2	17.2
3–4	14.8
5	8.1
6–9	32.4
10–12	18.9
Under 5	40.6
5–12	59.4
Total	100.0
Sample size[a]	1,751
Population estimate (in thousands)	11,972

Source: National Child Care Survey, 1990—Low-Income Study.
a. The base or denominator on which the percentages were calculated.

TABLE 2.2

Types of Low-Income Households with Children
Under Age 13, by Age of Youngest Child

Household Type	Under Age 5 (%)	Ages 5–12 (%)	Total
Two parents	42.1	26.6	35.3
Dual employed	10.2	8.0	9.3
One employed	23.6	13.8	19.3
0 employed	8.2	4.9	6.8
Single mother	53.1	63.9	57.9
Employed	18.4	35.5	25.9
Nonemployed	34.7	28.4	32.0
Single father	0.8	2.9	1.7
No parent	4.0	6.6	5.1
Total	100.0	100.0	100.0
Sample size[a]	546	427	973
Population estimate (in thousands)	3,735	2,198	6,653

Source: NCCS 1990—Low-Income Study.
Note: Percentages may not sum to 100, and sample frequencies may not sum to total sample size because of rounding.
a. The base or denominator on which the percentages were calculated.

342,000 families), neither the mother nor the father was present in the household.

Maternal Employment, Education, and Training Status

In 1990, fewer low-income mothers with children under age 13 were working for wages (42 percent) than were not employed (58 percent, not shown). Among low-income mothers who were employed in 1990, 55 percent were employed 35 hours or more per week (i.e., full-time), with no real variation by age of their youngest child. Yet almost 15 percent of mothers not currently working for wages were enrolled in an education or job training program. Thus 10 percent of low-income mothers whose youngest child was under age 5 and almost 7 percent of low-income mothers whose youngest child was of school age were actively participating in education or training programs. These proportions represent over 500,000 U.S. households.

Other Characteristics

In 1990, 46 percent of low-income families with children under age 13 had only one child, 32 percent had two children, and 22 percent had three or more children in the family (not shown). Forty-eight percent of these low-income households were nonwhite families in 1990, with non-Hispanic black families comprising 32 percent and Hispanic families representing over 14 percent of these families. Approximately 63 percent of households with children under age 13 and with annual incomes under $15,000 lived below the federal poverty line. Another 16 percent of these households fell between 100 percent and 125 percent of the poverty line (i.e., near poverty). Nevertheless, only 12 percent of all low-income families with children under age 13 were currently receiving AFDC, and another 35 percent were not currently on AFDC but had received AFDC payments within the past year.

Appendix B details sample distributions and population estimates of all low-income children under age 13 by key characteristics.

Chapter Three

Care Arrangements among Low-Income Children

This report uses a broad definition of child care arrangements. We assume that all children spend the majority of
time with their parents or guardians. However, many parents
also rely on someone else to supplement the care they provide
for their children. These caregivers may be relatives, friends,
or a nonrelative in or out of the child's home. Parents may
use other arrangements for a variety of reasons. For example,
when employed parents are at work, they need to arrange for
the care of their children. Also, many parents, regardless of
employment, may place their children in child care programs
designed for enrichment purposes. Supplemental arrangements may be used infrequently or on a regular basis. Among
those relying on regular arrangements, families use different
types of care and for varying amounts of time; some use
supplemental care for just a few hours a week, whereas others
require such care for 40 or more hours per week. Some
children have one arrangement and some children rely on

several arrangements each week. All of these programs or activities are included as "child care arrangements" because they substitute for parental care. Child care arrangements may require payment by parents or may be partially or completely free to parents.

This chapter describes the "regular" child care arrangements of all low-income children under age 13.[1] Thus children, not families, are the unit of analysis. First, we focus on the degree to which low-income children are cared for exclusively by their parents. Second, we discuss the main arrangements of low-income children according to what their parents report. Third, we examine the degree to which children are cared for by grandparents as well as nonrelatives *at all* on a regular basis, not just as the arrangement for the greatest amount of time. Describing the *main* arrangements of children presents only one piece of the child care puzzle. To develop a comprehensive picture of child care arrangements, we needed to examine the extent to which parents rely on other people to care for their children on a "regular" basis, even if this care is only for one or two hours a week. A couple of hours a week may be a critical component of parents' continued employment and/or essential for their children's development and safety. Fourth, we detail the preschool and school enrollments of children aged 3 to 5, to document the degree to which low-income children participate in formal programs at early ages. Fifth, we look at the special arrangements used by school-age children—that is, self-care, lessons, sports, and club activities. Sixth, we examine multiple supplemental arrangements to highlight the idea that child care consists of a combination of arrangements for many children.

Exclusive Parental Care

A substantial number of children are cared for exclusively by their parents (either the mother or the father) without depending on other relatives or market care on a regular basis. In other words, these children do not use any regular form of supplemental care. Approximately 35 percent of low-income children under age 13 are cared for only by their parents (38 percent of those under age 5 and 33 percent of those aged 5 to 12—see figure 3.1). These proportions vary dramatically by family structure and parental employment status.

Household Type

Children in two-parent families are substantially more likely than children of single mothers to be cared for exclusively by their parents, regardless of the age of the child (figure 3.1). For example, 29 percent of children under age 5 whose mothers are single are cared for solely by their mother, whereas 52 percent of children under age 5 in two-parent families are cared for solely by their parents.

Moreover, nonemployed parents are more likely to care exclusively for their children, regardless of family structure. Among two-parent families, children with one or neither parent employed are more likely to be cared for solely by a parent than children of dual-employed parents (figure 3.2). Yet only about two-fifths of both preschool-age (40 percent) and school-age children (42 percent) from households headed by a nonemployed single mother are cared for solely by a parent.

Children of employed single mothers are least likely to be cared for solely by a parent, regardless of the child's age (figure 3.2). Most employed single mothers cannot easily share care with the child's absent father. However, dual-employed families may be able to juggle work schedules to care for their children themselves. Thus, among children under age 5, only 8 percent of those from households headed by an employed single mother are cared for exclusively by a parent, whereas nearly 22 percent of children from dual-employed households are cared for only by their parents (figure 3.2).

FIGURE 3.1

Percentage of Children Cared for Solely by Parent, by Family and Age of Child

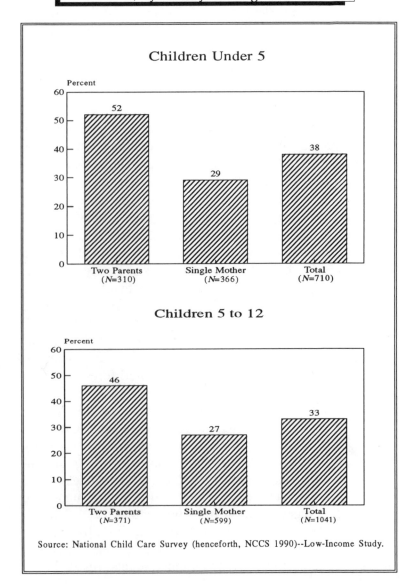

Source: National Child Care Survey (henceforth, NCCS 1990)--Low-Income Study.

FIGURE 3.2

Percentage of Children Cared for Solely by Parent, by Household Type and Age of Child

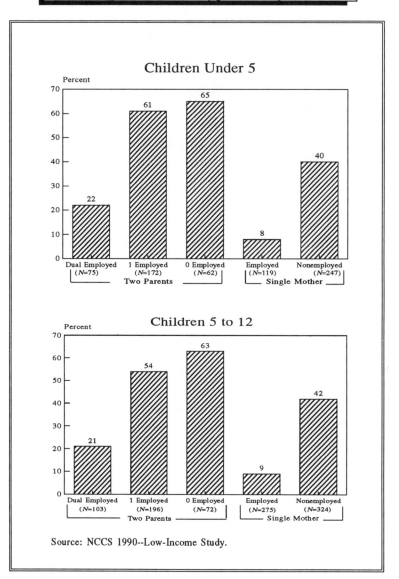

Source: NCCS 1990--Low-Income Study.

Maternal Employment, Education, and Training Status

Children with employed mothers or with nonemployed mothers in education or job training programs are less likely to be cared for exclusively by a parent than children of other nonemployed mothers, regardless of the age of the child (figure 3.3). Thus, participation in programs designed to enhance employment opportunities presents challenges similar to employment *per se* in how parents manage to care for their children. Of course, children under age 5 with full-time employed mothers (i.e., employed 35 or more hours per week) are least likely to be cared for solely by a parent (8 percent), compared to other low-income children.

Main Arrangements: Who Provides Care for the Greatest Amount of Time

Although parents are typically the primary providers of care, many families report that they rely on supplemental care. Since children may be in multiple arrangements, and since some experiences may consist of relatively brief periods with a provider, the NCCS asked respondents to complete a time diary of child care arrangements for up to four children under age 13 in the family. The main arrangement is the one used the most hours per week. If a child did not use any supplemental care, the main arrangement is care by the parents. In this report, "parent" as a main arrangement includes children exclusively cared for by a parent as well as children using some supplemental care. This makes the definition of the category compatible with previous studies of primary child care arrangements.

School is the primary activity and form of care for school-age children. Unlike previous studies that have included

FIGURE 3.3

Percentage of Children Cared for Solely by Parent, by Maternal Employment, Education, and Training, and Age of Child

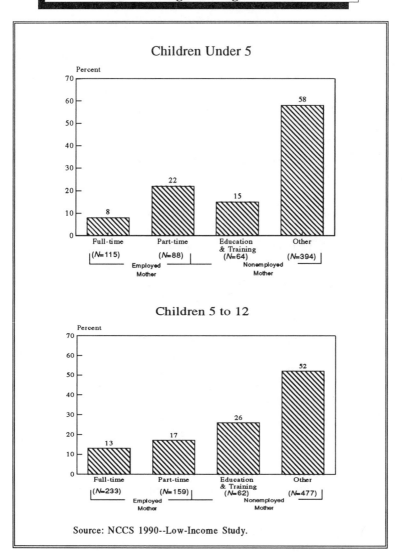

Children Under 5

Percent

Full-time	Part-time	Education & Training	Other
8	22	15	58
(N=115)	(N=88)	(N=64)	(N=394)
	Employed Mother		Nonemployed Mother

Children 5 to 12

Percent

Full-time	Part-time	Education & Training	Other
13	17	26	52
(N=233)	(N=159)	(N=62)	(N=477)
	Employed Mother		Nonemployed Mother

Source: NCCS 1990--Low-Income Study.

school as a form of child care, we have excluded it from our analysis of main arrangements because not everyone reports school as an arrangement, even if the child is enrolled in school and the parent works during school hours. We assume all school-age children are enrolled in school, and report only their nonschool arrangements.

Based on the child-care time diaries, figure 3.4 shows that 48 percent of low-income children under age 5 are taken care of mainly by their parents (i.e., for the greatest amount of hours per week). Mothers are more likely to be the main care provider than fathers; among low-income children under age 5 who are reported to have parents as their main arrangement, 75 percent are mainly taken care of by their mother, whereas 25 percent are mainly taken care of by their father (not shown). In other words, 12 percent of all low-income children under age 5 are reported to be cared for by their father as their main arrangement (not shown).

Low-income children under age 5 are just as likely to be in the care of a relative (22 percent) as to be in the care of a nonrelative (25 percent, not shown) for their reported main arrangement (figure 3.4). In this study, as in the main NCCS report, care by a relative includes grandparents, siblings, aunts/uncles, and cousins. Grandparents are a predominant source of relative care; nearly 17 percent of all low-income children under age 5 are cared for mainly by a grandparent (not shown). In the category of nonrelative care, just under 15 percent of low-income children under age 5 are in centers, 8 percent are in family day care homes, and only 2 percent are cared for by a nonrelative in the child's home as the main arrangement. The remaining children under age 5 (6 percent) are reported to be in other main arrangements (i.e., lessons, sports, clubs, or self-care).

The pattern is similar for children aged 5 to 12. Nearly 48 percent of school-age children are reported to be in parental care as the main arrangement, whereas 20 percent are in the care of another relative and 14 percent are in the care of a nonrelative (figure 3.4). Like preschool-age children, school-

FIGURE 3.4

Main Arrangement by Age of Child

Children Under 5

Parent, 48%

In-Home, 2%

Relative, 22%

FDC, 8%

Other, 6%

Center, 15%

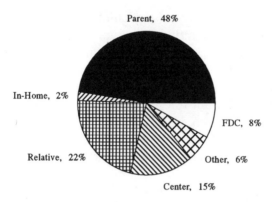

Children 5 to 12

Parent, 48%

In-Home, 4%

Relative, 20%

FDC, 4%

Other, 19%

Center, 6%

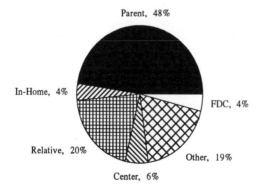

Source: NCCS 1990--Low-Income Study.

age children are more likely to be cared for mainly by their mother than by their father; 21 percent of school-age children with parental care as their main arrangement are primarily cared for by their father (not shown). In other words, 10 percent of all low-income children aged 5 to 12 have fathers as their main caregiver (not shown). Grandparents also care for school-age children; 11 percent of low-income children aged 5 to 12 use grandparents as their main arrangement (not shown).

The percentage of school-age children in nonrelative care does not vary significantly by the type of nonrelative care: 6 percent are in centers, 4 percent are in family day care homes, and 4 percent are cared for in their own home (figure 3.4). However, other arrangements such as lessons and self-care play a more important role for school-age children than for preschool-age children. Nearly 19 percent of school-age children are in these other arrangements as the reported *main* form of care. We discuss these other arrangements in a later section.

The degree to which parents report that they are the *main* providers, though not necessarily the only providers of care, and the proportion of children in a main nonparental arrangement vary by family structure and parental employment status for both preschool-age and school-age children.

Parental Care

Low-income parents are more likely to be the reported main arrangement for children in two-parent families and in families headed by a nonemployed single mother than for children of employed single mothers (table 3.1). Moreover, low-income parents are more likely to be the main caregivers for children with nonemployed mothers who are *not* in education or training programs than is the case for other low-income children (table 3.2). This pattern is most evident for low-income children under age 5.

TABLE 3.1

Main Arrangement by Household Type for Preschool and School-Age Children

	Parent (%)	Relative (%)	In-Home (%)	FDC[a] (%)	Center (%)	Other (%)	Total (%)	Sample Size[b]
Children Under 5								
Two parents								
Dual employed	64.1	15.8	1.5	5.5	8.5	4.6	100	310
One employed	40.2	26.7	0.8	11.0	12.1	9.3	100	75
0 employed	69.2	15.4	2.3	4.3	5.2	3.6	100	172
Single mother	79.0	3.9	0.0	2.3	13.2	1.6	100	62
Employed	37.7	25.7	2.4	9.9	20.3	3.8	100	366
Nonemployed	16.9	30.1	1.0	21.0	27.2	3.8	100	119
Total	47.8	23.7	3.1	4.6	17.0	3.8	100	247
	47.5	22.2	2.0	7.8	14.7	5.8	100	710
Children 5 to 12								
Two parents								
Dual employed	64.5	13.2	1.1	3.0	4.1	14.1	100	371
One employed	41.5	29.1	2.1	4.8	4.9	17.4	100	103
0 employed	73.0	7.7	0.4	3.1	2.3	13.5	100	196
Single mother	74.0	5.6	1.6	0.0	7.9	10.6	100	72
Employed	42.2	24.5	4.9	5.6	6.8	15.9	100	599
Nonemployed	24.9	35.9	7.2	9.8	7.3	14.9	100	275
Total	56.9	14.9	3.0	2.1	6.3	16.8	100	324
	47.8	19.9	3.6	4.4	5.6	18.7	100	1,041

Source: NCCS 1990—Low-Income Study.
Note: Totals include children in single-father and no-parent households.
a. FDC, family day care.
b. The base or denominator on which the percentages were calculated.

Relative Care

Care by a relative is especially prevalent for low-income children with single mothers and with employed mothers, especially those in dual-employed families. For example, among children under age 5, 27 percent of those in dual-employed families are mainly cared for by a relative (table 3.1). Like employed mothers, nonemployed mothers in education or training programs also rely on relatives as the main caregivers. About 23 percent of children under age 5, and 14 percent of children aged 5 to 12 whose mothers are in education or training programs, are mainly cared for by a relative (table 3.2).

Nonrelative Care

Few low-income children are primarily cared for in their own home by a nonrelative, regardless of the age of the child. This is also the case across children of all incomes (Hofferth et al. 1991). Family day care homes and centers serve as the main arrangement for many low-income children, especially children under age 5. In particular, children under age 5 are more likely to be enrolled either in family day care or in center-based care if the family is headed by a single employed mother than are children in other low-income families (table 3.1). Moreover, children under age 5 whose mothers are not employed but are in education or training programs are more likely to be in center-based care (35 percent) than in any other type of main arrangement (table 3.2).

The distribution of main arrangements among low-income children varies little by family income, poverty status, or AFDC receipt, after family structure and parental employment status are held constant.

Time Spent in Supplemental Care

Among low-income children whose main arrangement is a form of supplemental care, children under age 5 spend almost 28

TABLE 3.2

Main Arrangement by Maternal Employment, Education, and Training Status for Preschool and School-Age Children

	Parent (%)	Relative (%)	In-Home (%)	FDC[a] (%)	Center (%)	Other (%)	Total (%)	Sample Size[b]
Children Under 5								
Employed mother	26.2	28.3	1.4	16.5	23.6	4.1	100	280
Full-time	20.9	32.3	1.4	17.2	23.1	5.2	100	115
Part-time	30.8	23.5	0.7	20.2	18.5	6.4	100	88
Nonemployed mother	60.9	17.2	2.4	3.4	12.5	3.6	100	458
Education and training	26.2	23.3	2.7	12.6	35.1	0.0	100	64
Other	66.5	16.2	2.4	1.9	8.8	4.2	100	394
Children 5 to 12								
Employed mother	35.0	29.9	5.2	8.5	6.8	14.5	100	489
Full-time	30.7	33.9	5.6	11.7	7.9	10.3	100	233
Part-time	39.0	26.6	5.6	4.6	4.6	19.5	100	159
Nonemployed mother	64.2	10.8	2.2	1.7	5.3	15.8	100	539
Education and training	45.3	14.3	6.0	9.2	9.9	15.2	100	62
Other	66.7	10.3	1.7	0.7	4.7	15.9	100	477

Source: NCCS 1990—Low-Income Study.
Note: Totals include children in single-father and no-parent households.
a. FDC, family day care.
b. The base or denominator on which the percentages were calculated.

hours per week, and children aged 5 to 12 spend about 13 hours per week on average in this supplemental arrangement. Table 3.3 separates the mean number of hours in supplemental care as a main arrangement by whether or not the care is provided by a relative or a nonrelative, the age of child, and household type.

The amount of time that preschool-age children spend in a supplemental main arrangement varies by family structure and parental employment status. Overall, young children in two-parent families spend less time in a supplemental main arrangement than children in families headed by a single mother (22 versus 29 hours per week, respectively; see table 3.3). However, children under age 5 of dual-employed parents spend more time in supplemental care than comparable children of single nonemployed mothers (30 versus 21 hours per week, respectively). Children under age 5 of employed single mothers spend, on average, the greatest number of hours in a supplemental arrangement (38 hours per week). Moreover, these children spend a greater amount of time in relative care (45 hours) compared with nonrelative care (34 hours). There is no significant difference in time spent in relative versus nonrelative care among children under age 5 in two-parent families (23 versus 22 hours per week, respectively).

Among children aged 5 to 12, there are no significant differences in the amount of time spent in relative care by household type. However, school-age children cared for primarily by a nonrelative spend fewer hours in a supplemental main arrangement than school-age children relying on relatives. Moreover, children of employed single mothers spend more hours in nonrelative care on average than other children.

There are no meaningful differences in the average number of hours in a supplemental main arrangement by family income, poverty status, or AFDC receipt, after controlling for maternal employment status.

TABLE 3.3

Mean Hours per Week in Nonparental Main Arrangement by Household Type for Preschool and School-Age Children

	Relative		Nonrelative		Total	
	Mean	N[b]	Mean	N[b]	Mean	N[b]
Children Under 5						
Two parents	22.5	49	21.9	61	22.2	110
Dual employed	29.2	20	30.6	24	30.0	44
One employed	18.6	26	18.4	27	18.5	53
0 employed	*[a]	2	11.1	11	10.9	13
Single mother	28.4	94	28.9	128	28.7	222
Employed	45.0	36	34.0	63	38.0	99
Nonemployed	18.3	58	23.8	65	21.2	123
Total	27.3	157	28.1	198	27.8	355
Children 5 to 12						
Two parents	14.1	49	7.8	81	10.2	130
Dual employed	14.0	30	8.4	29	11.3	59
One employed	16.3	15	7.8	38	10.3	53
0 employed	*[a]	4	6.7	14	6.5	18
Single mother	15.7	147	12.0	198	13.6	345
Employed	15.6	99	14.3	108	14.9	206
Nonemployed	15.8	48	9.3	90	11.6	138
Total	16.2	207	11.4	297	13.4	504

Source: NCCS 1990—Low-Income Study.
a. Asterisk (*) denotes fewer than 10 cases.
b. Total number of children in this category.

Role of Grandparents as Caregivers

Grandparents play a valuable role as caregivers for many children. Thus we also examined the proportion of children relying on any care *at all* by a grandparent on a "regular" basis (i.e., at least once a week for the two weeks previous), regardless of the amount of time spent in care. Looking at care arrangements in this way helped us assess the extent of care provided by grandparents.

First, younger children are more likely to be in the care of a grandparent than are older children. Twenty-nine percent of children under age 5 and 20 percent of children aged 5 to 12 are cared for by their grandparents *at all* on a regular basis (figure 3.5). Recall that 17 percent of children under age 5 and 11 percent of children aged 5 to 12 use grandparents as their *main* arrangement (not shown). Thus many preschool-age and school-age children use grandparents as either a secondary or tertiary arrangement.

Second, the proportion of low-income children cared for by grandparents varies by household type, maternal employment, and poverty status.

Household Type

Children of single mothers are more likely to be cared for by their grandparents than children in two-parent families. Approximately 35 percent of children under age 5 whose mothers are single are cared for by a grandparent, compared with 20 percent of those in two-parent families (figure 3.5).

When we looked at parental employment in conjunction with family structure, we found that grandparents play an important caregiving role for children in dual-employed families, in addition to families of single mothers. For example, 43 percent of children under age 5 of employed single mothers and 35 percent of those in dual-employed families rely on grandparents to provide care on a regular basis (figure 3.6).

FIGURE 3.5

> ### Percentage of Children Cared for by a Grandparent, by Family Structure and Age of Child

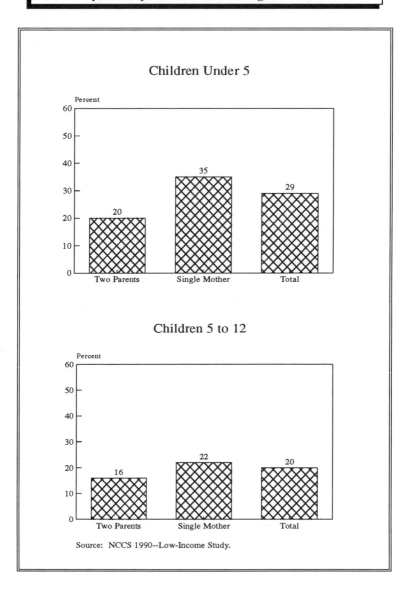

Source: NCCS 1990--Low-Income Study.

FIGURE 3.6

Percentage of Children Under Age 5 Cared for
by a Grandparent, by Household Type

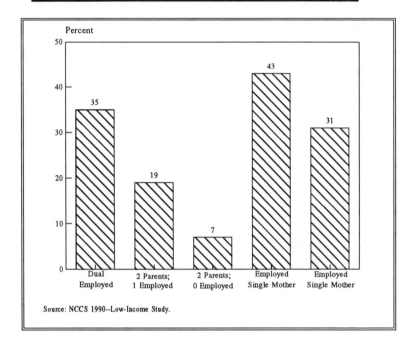

Source: NCCS 1990--Low-Income Study.

The same basic pattern of usage is found among low-income
children aged 5 to 12 (figure 3.7).

Maternal Employment, Education, and Training Status

Although grandparents are the predominant source of supplemental care for both younger and older children with full-time
employed mothers, children under age 5 with nonemployed
mothers in education and training programs are also often
cared for by a grandparent on a regular basis (34 percent;
figure 3.8). School-age children with nonemployed mothers

FIGURE 3.7

Percentage of Children Ages 5 to 12 Cared for
by a Grandparent, by Household Type

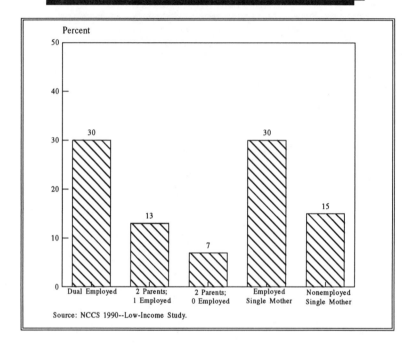

are less likely to be cared for by a grandparent than those with full-time employed mothers (figure 3.9). There is no significant difference in use of grandparent care based on education and training status among children of nonemployed mothers.

Poverty Status

Among these low-income families, there are no significant differences in the proportion of children being cared for by a grandparent on a regular basis by poverty status, regardless of the age of the child (figure 3.10).

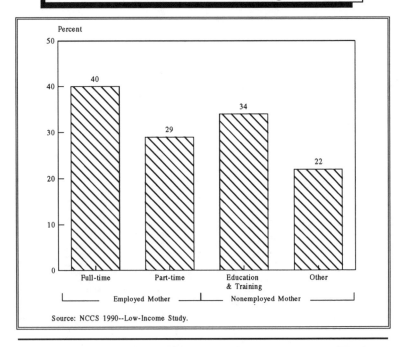

FIGURE 3.8

Percentage of Children Under Age 5 Cared for by a Grandparent, by Maternal Employment, Education, and Training

Source: NCCS 1990--Low-Income Study.

Role of Nonrelatives: In-Home Providers, Family Day Care Homes, and Centers

This section assesses the degree to which nonrelatives provide any care *at all* for low-income children on a regular basis. We examine three types of nonrelative care: in-home providers, family day care homes, and centers. Center-based care includes enrollment in Head Start for children under age 5.

Centers play the greatest role in nonrelative care, especially for younger children. Centers provide regular care for

FIGURE 3.9

Percentage of Children Ages 5 to 12 Cared for by a Grandparent, by Maternal Employment, Education, and Training

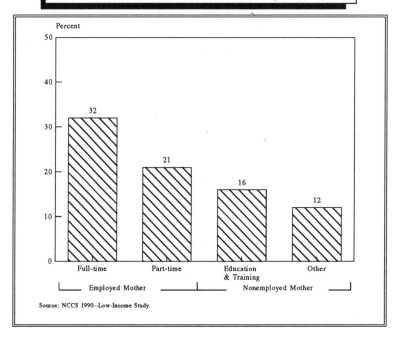

Source: NCCS 1990--Low-Income Study.

almost 20 percent of children under age 5, and some proportion of time on a weekly basis for 10 percent of children aged 5 to 12 (figure 3.11). Recall that 15 percent of low-income children under age 5 rely on center care as their *main* arrangement (figure 3.4, table 3.1). Family day care homes are a more prevalent source of care for younger children than for older children. Twelve percent of children under age 5 are in a family day care home at some time during the week, whereas only 6 percent of children aged 5 to 12 spend time with a family day care provider on a regular basis (figure 3.11). In comparison, 8 percent of preschool-age children and 4 percent of school-age children use family day care as a *main* arrangement (table 3.1).

FIGURE 3.10

Percentage of Children Cared for by a Grandparent,
by Poverty Status and Age of Child

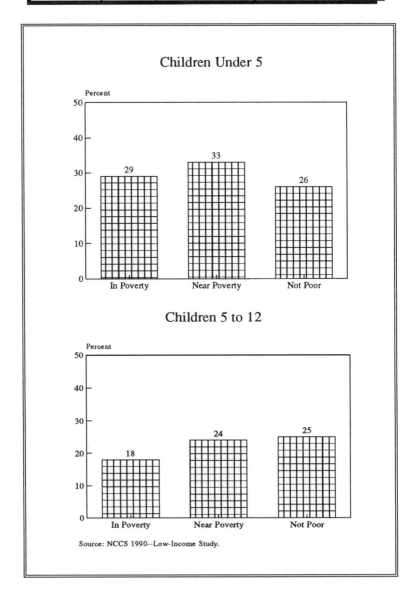

Children Under 5

Children 5 to 12

Source: NCCS 1990--Low-Income Study.

FIGURE 3.11

Percentage of Children Relying on Any Nonrelative Care, by Family Structure and Age of Child

Children Under 5

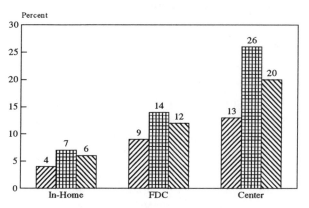

Children 5 to 12

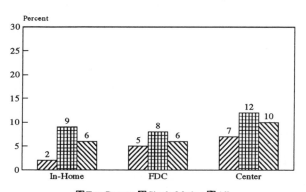

Source: NCCS 1990--Low-Income Study
Note: Children may be in multiple arrangements.

Few low-income children are cared for by a nonrelative in their own home at all, regardless of the age of the child. Approximately 6 percent of children under age 13 use an in-home provider *at all* (figure 3.11). Though not statistically significant, this figure is somewhat higher than the proportion who rely on in-home care as their *main* arrangement (4 percent; see table 3.1).

Reliance on nonrelative care also varies by household type, maternal employment, and poverty status.

Household Type

Regardless of the age of the child, children of single mothers are slightly more likely to be cared for by a nonrelative in their own home, in another home, or in a center than children in two-parent families (figure 3.11). When we disaggregated by parental employment status, we found no significant difference in use of an in-home provider among children under age 5 (figure 3.12). However, school-age children in families headed by an employed single mother are significantly more likely to use in-home nonrelative care than are school-age children in two-parent families (12 percent versus 1–4 percent, respectively; figure 3.13).

Both younger and older children are more likely to be in family day care homes and centers if their mothers are employed and single than are children in other household types (figures 3.12 and 3.13). Center-based care and family day care homes are especially important for preschool-age children of employed single mothers—37 percent of these children are in centers on a regular basis, and 27 percent are in family day care homes (figure 3.12).

Maternal Employment, Education, and Training Status

Only a slightly higher proportion of low-income children of full-time employed mothers are cared for by a nonrelative at some time during the week than those with part-time em-

FIGURE 3.12

Percentage of Children Under Age 5 Relying on Any
Nonrelative Care, by Household Type

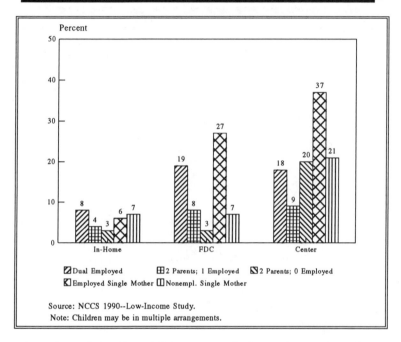

Source: NCCS 1990--Low-Income Study.
Note: Children may be in multiple arrangements.

ployed mothers. In addition, nonrelatives play a significant
role in caring for both younger and older children of nonemployed mothers enrolled in education and training programs
(figures 3.14 and 3.15). This pattern is most evident among
children under age 5: 45 percent of those with nonemployed
mothers in education and training use center care, compared
to 33 percent of those with full-time employed mothers
(figure 3.14).

Poverty Status

Children whose family income lies below the federal poverty
line are significantly less likely than other low-income chil-

FIGURE 3.13

Percentage of Children Ages 5 to 12 Relying on
Any Nonrelative Care, by Household Type

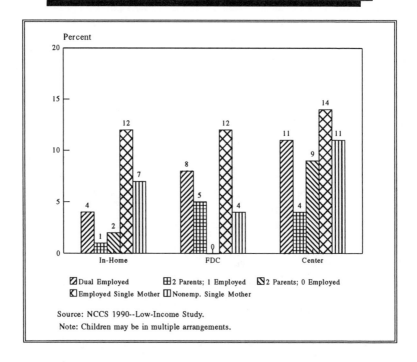

Source: NCCS 1990--Low-Income Study.
Note: Children may be in multiple arrangements.

dren to be enrolled in family day care homes and centers *at
all*, especially if the child is of school age (figure 3.16). For
example, only 7 percent of school-age children in poverty are
in center care and only 5 percent are in family day care homes
on a regular basis, compared to 22 percent of children in
families with annual incomes between 100 percent and 125
percent of the federal poverty line (i.e., near poor) who use
centers (7 percent are in family day care). There is no significant difference in enrollments in family day care homes or
centers among children under age 5.

FIGURE 3.14

Percentage of Children Under Age 5 Relying
on Any Nonrelative Care, by Maternal
Employment, Education, and Training

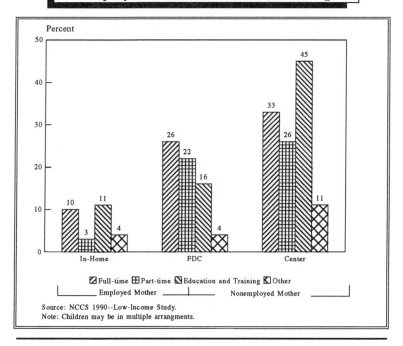

Source: NCCS 1990--Low-Income Study.
Note: Children may be in multiple arrangments.

Preschool and School Enrollments for Children Aged 3 to 5

Preschool programs providing compensatory education and social services to low-income children prepare them for school entry. This section details enrollments in Head Start, center-based programs, and kindergarten or first grade (i.e., school) for all low-income children aged 3 to 5. Enrollments in these three types of programs are not mutually exclusive, because children may attend multiple programs. For example, a child may be in both Head Start and a center-based program, or just in Head Start. Therefore, we also examined enroll-

FIGURE 3.15

Percentage of Children Ages 5 to 12 Relying
on Any Nonrelative Care, by Maternal
Employment, Education and Training

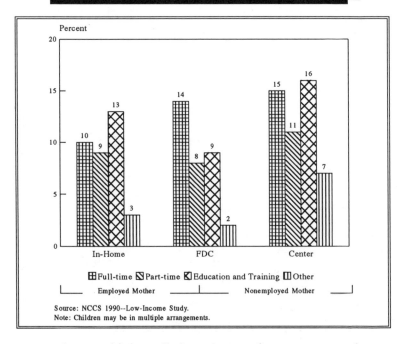

Source: NCCS 1990--Low-Income Study.
Note: Children may be in multiple arrangements.

ments by combining all three types of arrangements into a
fourth category: enrollment in Head Start *or* a center-based
program *or* school. This fourth category is a summary indicator of enrollment in at least one of these programs.

Age of Child

About 55 percent of all low-income children aged 3 to 5 are
enrolled in Head Start, a center-based program, or school.
Older children are more likely than younger children to be in at
least one of these programs (figure 3.17). Nearly all 5-year-olds
(83 percent) are enrolled in a preschool program, with the

FIGURE 3.16

Percentage of Children Relying on Any Nonrelative Care, by Poverty Status and Age of Child

Children Under 5

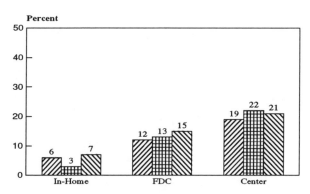

In Poverty ⊞ Near Poverty ◩ Not Poor

Children 5 to 12

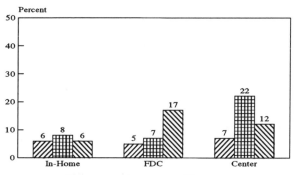

In Poverty ⊞ Near Poverty ◩ Not Poor

Source: NCCS 1990--Low-Income Study.
Note: Children may be in multiple arrangements.

FIGURE 3.17

Percentage of Enrollments in Head Start,
School, and Center-Based Programs for All
3–5-Year-Olds, by Age of Child

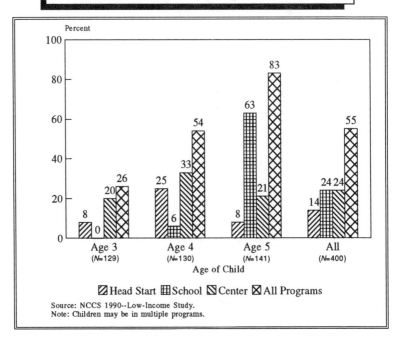

Source: NCCS 1990--Low-Income Study.
Note: Children may be in multiple programs.

majority in school, whereas only 26 percent of 3-year-olds
are enrolled in any program. Four-year-olds are most likely
to be in a center-based program (33 percent) or in Head Start
(25 percent).

Household Type

Low-income children of single mothers are more likely to be
in at least one of these programs than those in two-parent
families (62 percent compared to 46 percent, respectively; see
figure 3.18). This pattern holds even when parental employment status is taken into account. Moreover, children of
employed single mothers are more likely to be enrolled in a

FIGURE 3.18

Percentage of Enrollments in Head Start,
School, and Center-Based Programs for
All 3–5-Year-Olds, by Family Structure

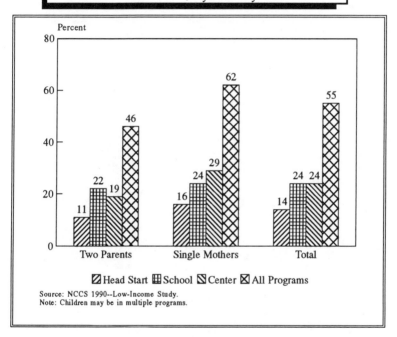

Source: NCCS 1990--Low-Income Study.
Note: Children may be in multiple programs.

center-based program than other low-income children (figure 3.19). Children in two-parent families where neither parent is employed and children of nonemployed single mothers are more likely to be enrolled in Head Start than other low-income children aged 3 to 5.

Maternal Employment, Education, and Training Status

Low-income children whose mothers participate in an education or job training program are more likely than other low-income children to be enrolled in a preschool program, because they are more likely to be enrolled in Head Start (30 percent;

FIGURE 3.19

Percentage of Enrollments in Head Start,
School, and Center-Based Programs for
All 3–5-Year-Olds, by Household Type

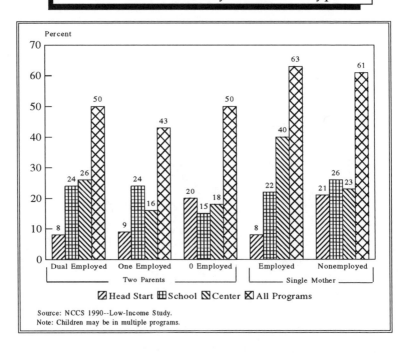

Source: NCCS 1990--Low-Income Study.
Note: Children may be in multiple programs.

see figure 3.20). Children with either full-time or part-time employed mothers are less likely to be enrolled in Head Start (8 percent and 6 percent, respectively) than are other low-income children. Children with mothers who are *not* employed and who are *not* in an education or training program are least likely to be in a center-based program.

AFDC Receipt and Maternal Employment Status

Children in families receiving AFDC currently (at the time of the NCCS) or during the past year are more likely to be enrolled in Head Start than children in non-AFDC families,

FIGURE 3.20

Percentage of Enrollments in Head Start, School, and Center-Based Programs for All 3–5-Year-Olds, by Maternal Employment Status

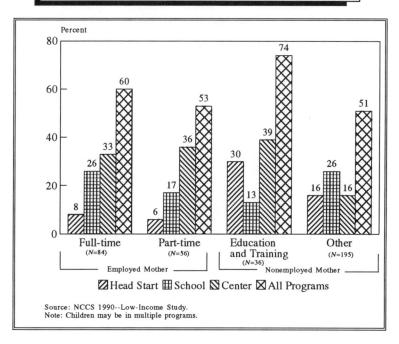

Source: NCCS 1990--Low-Income Study.
Note: Children may be in multiple programs.

regardless of their mother's employment status (figure 3.21). Enrollment in center-based programs was highest among children of AFDC mothers in employment or education/training. Children of nonemployed mothers who are *not* currently receiving AFDC are far less likely than other children to attend a center-based program.

Poverty Status and Race/Ethnicity

Low-income children living in poverty (i.e., family income below the federal poverty line) or near the poverty level (i.e., family income between 100 percent and 125 percent of the

FIGURE 3.21

Percentage of Enrollments in Head Start, School, and Center-Based Programs for all 3–5-Year-Olds, by AFDC Receipt and Maternal Employment

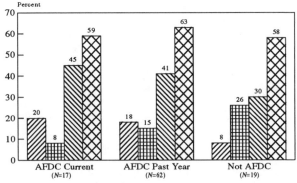

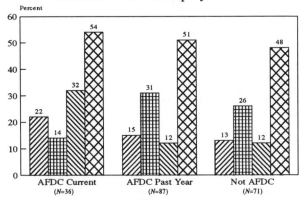

Source: NCCS 1990--Low-Income Study.
Note: Children may be in multiple programs.

Care Arrangements among Low-Income Children ■ *49*

FIGURE 3.22

Percentage of Enrollments in Head Start for All 3–5-
Year-Olds, by Poverty Status and Age of Child

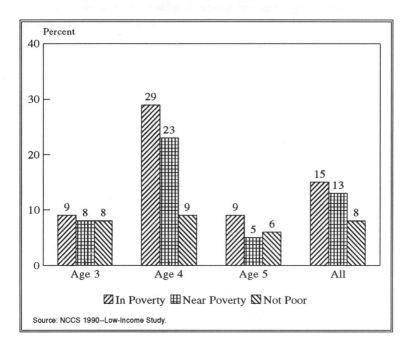

Source: NCCS 1990--Low-Income Study.

poverty line) are more likely to be enrolled in Head Start (15
percent and 13 percent, respectively) than low-income children living 25 percent or more above the poverty level (8
percent; see figure 3.22). Because of small sample sizes, these
differences are not statistically significant. Head Start enrollments are highest among 4-year-olds in poverty (29 percent)
or near poverty (23 percent).

Although both black and Hispanic low-income children
are more likely to be enrolled in Head Start (21 percent and
18 percent, respectively) than white low-income children (8
percent), Hispanic children are less likely to attend a center-
based program (17 percent) than either black children (24

FIGURE 3.23

Percentage of Enrollments in Head Start,
School, and Center-Based Programs for
3–5-Year-Olds in Poverty, by Race/Ethnicity

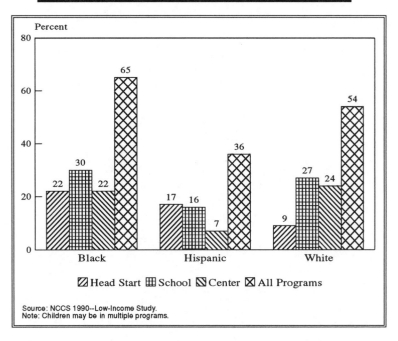

Source: NCCS 1990--Low-Income Study.
Note: Children may be in multiple programs.

percent) or white children (26 percent; not shown). Figure 3.23 indicates that differences in enrollments by race/ethnicity remain after controlling for poverty status: 22 percent of black children in poverty and 17 percent of Hispanic children in poverty compared to 9 percent of poor white children in poverty are enrolled in Head Start.

Arrangements for School-Age Children

The nature of child care arrangements changes as children grow older. Many parents use lessons, sports, and club activities as a way to cover the care of older children after school as well as to expand their children's academic, physical, social, and cultural training. Parents also leave more school-age children alone to take care of themselves.

Lessons, Sports, and Clubs

Although only 11 percent of all low-income children of school age rely specifically on lessons, sports, or clubs as a *main* arrangement, about 30 percent take lessons or participate in sports or club activities on a "regular" weekly basis. Family structure and parental employment do not significantly determine school-age children's extracurricular activities (see table 3.4). A family's standard of living, not simply whether or not the mother is employed, influences children's extracurricular activities. Thus, a lower percentage of children in poverty (28 percent) regularly take lessons or participate in sports or club activities than other low-income children (40 percent of children living in near poverty and 38 percent of nonpoor, low-income children).

Self-Care

Only 2 percent of school-age children in low-income families take care of themselves as their reported *main* arrangement (not shown), whereas almost 9 percent are in self-care for some period of time on a "regular" weekly basis (table 3.4). There are no statistically significant differences in the percentage of low-income children taking care of themselves by household type, maternal employment, or poverty status.

Use of Multiple Supplemental Arrangements

Earlier in this chapter we reported that many parents are the sole providers of care for their children. However, 62 percent

TABLE 3.4

Percentage of School-Age Children in Lessons
and Self-Care

	Lessons	Self-Care	Sample Size[a]
Household Type			
Two parents	28.8	8.3	371
Dual employed	35.9	8.0	103
One employed	25.3	9.1	196
0 employed	27.9	6.7	72
Single mother	31.9	9.0	599
Employed	35.5	11.7	275
Nonemployed	28.7	6.7	324
Maternal Employment			
Employed mother	34.5	9.8	427
Full-time	36.2	9.5	233
Part-time	33.1	12.1	159
Nonemployed mother	27.6	8.0	539
Education and training	29.8	7.3	62
Other	36.7	8.1	477
Poverty Status			
Poor	28.1	8.8	760
Near poor	40.1	10.6	134
Not poor	38.2	5.9	115
Total	30.1	8.5	1,041

Source: NCCS 1990—Low-Income Study.
Note: Children may be in multiple arrangements, and totals
for employed mothers include unknown hours worked per week.
a. The base or denominator on which these percentages were calculated.

of children under age 5 and 67 percent of children aged 5 to
12 are cared for by someone other than a parent on a regular
basis each week (not shown). This section examines the

degree to which low-income children rely on *more than one* supplemental arrangement on a "regular" weekly basis. For example, parents may use both center-based care and relative care in addition to the care they provide for children themselves. For some parents, balancing employment and child care responsibilities is quite complicated. Even for parents who are not employed, we found that child care may consist of a combination of arrangements.

First, there is little difference between preschool-age and school-age children in the degree to which they rely on more than one supplemental arrangement. Among low-income families, about 24 percent of children under age 5 and 28 percent of school-age children are in more than one supplemental arrangement on a regular basis (figure 3.24). Second, family characteristics are more important than the age of the child in determining the use of multiple supplemental arrangements. For example, children of single mothers are substantially more likely to use more than one supplemental arrangement than children of two-parent families, regardless of the age of the child (figure 3.24).

Household Type

Parental employment in conjunction with family structure is especially relevant to the number of supplemental arrangements used by low-income children. Children in two-parent families where at least one parent is not employed are least likely to rely on more than one supplemental arrangement, regardless of the age of the child (figure 3.25). Although it is not surprising that a high proportion of children in families headed by an employed single mother are in more than one supplemental arrangement (45 percent of children under age 5 and 47 percent of children aged 5 to 12), many single mothers who are *not* working for wages also place their children in multiple supplemental arrangements (24 percent of children in both age groups).

FIGURE 3.24

Percentage of Children in Multiple Nonparental
Arrangements, by Family Structure and Age of Child

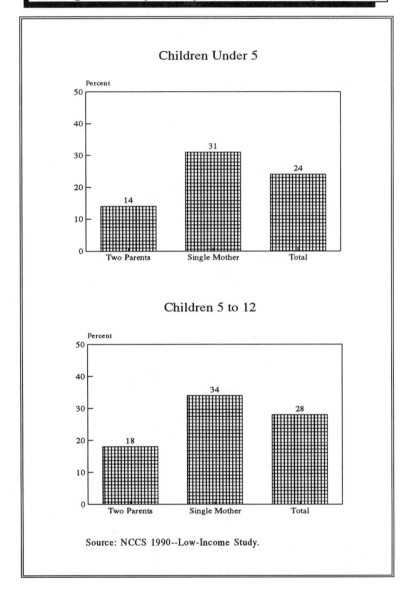

Source: NCCS 1990--Low-Income Study.

FIGURE 3.25

Percentage of Children in Multiple Nonparental Arrangements, by Household Type and Age of Child

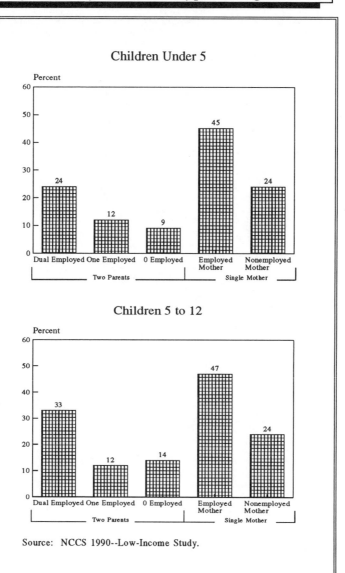

Source: NCCS 1990--Low-Income Study.

FIGURE 3.26

Percentage of Children in Multiple Nonparental
Arrangements, by Maternal Employment,
Education, and Training, and Age of Child

Children Under 5

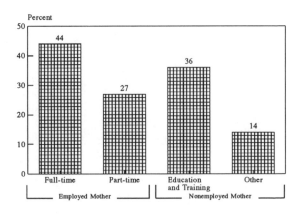

Children 5 to 12

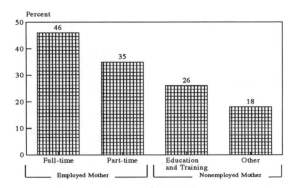

Source: NCCS 1990--Low-Income Study.

TABLE 3.5

Percentage of Children in Multiple Nonparental Arrangements by Poverty Status, AFDC Receipt, Family Size, and Main Arrangement

| | Children Under Age 5 | | | | Children Ages 5 to 12 | | | |
| | "Employed" Mother[a] | | Nonemployed Mother | | "Employed" Mother[a] | | Nonemployed Mother | |
	%	N[b]	%	N[b]	%	N[b]	%	N[b]
Poverty Status								
Poor	38.1	182	15.9	277	35.3	17	18.6	387
Near poor	25.3	49	15.2	50	49.9	90	15.0	42
Not poor	37.6	49	9.2	50	40.3	76	19.7	29
AFDC[c] Receipt								
Current	45.2	21	13.9	77	21.8	37	16.1	93
Past year	30.3	107	15.0	160	47.0	109	20.5	217
Not AFDC	38.1	152	13.7	157	37.4	343	16.0	167
Children Under 13								
1 child	49.3	88	15.7	94	46.9	146	15.7	77
2 children	37.1	109	14.5	139	35.0	182	21.4	159
3 or more children	19.7	84	13.2	162	34.4	161	16.7	242
Main Arrangement								
Parent	16.0	73	3.5	262	20.6	171	4.3	318
Relative	41.2	79	31.3	64	52.1	146	57.8	49
In-Home	*d	4	*d	9	54.6	16	*d	8
FDC[e]	25.4	46	*d	7	48.7	41	*d	3
Center	59.0	66	60.9	35	46.5	33	67.5	23
Other	32.9	12	7.5	17	37.2	71	28.0	76
Total	35.7	280	14.3	394	38.4	489	18.1	477

Source: NCCS 1990—Low-Income Study.
a. "Employed" mothers includes those in education and training programs.
b. The base or denominator on which these percentages were calculated.
c. AFDC, Aid to Families with Dependent Children.
d. Asterisk (*) denotes fewer than 10 cases.
e. FDC, family day care.

Maternal Employment, Education, and Training Status

Regardless of the age of the child, children of full-time employed mothers are more likely to be in more than one supplemental arrangement than children of part-time employed mothers or children of nonemployed mothers (figure 3.26). Among children with nonemployed mothers, a higher proportion of those with mothers in education and training programs are in multiple arrangements than is the case for those with mothers not in these programs. This gap is even larger for children under age 5. For example, 44 percent of children under age 5 with full-time employed mothers, 27 percent of those with part-time employed mothers, 36 percent of those with nonemployed mothers in education or training programs, and 14 percent of those with other nonemployed mothers are in more than one supplemental arrangement.

Thus the demands of education and training programs are similar to the demands of employment in terms of arranging for the care of children. This finding suggests that not all nonemployed mothers are available for full-time parental care. Some mothers not currently working for wages are engaged in activities that enhance their employment opportunities. Therefore we combined employed mothers with nonemployed mothers in education and training programs to contrast them with other nonemployed mothers not in education and training programs according to other key characteristics.

Other Family Characteristics

The proportion of children in more than one supplemental arrangement varies little by poverty status, after age of child and maternal employment status are held constant (see table 3.5). Although there is no meaningful difference by AFDC receipt among children with nonemployed mothers *not* in education and training programs, school-age children in families currently receiving AFDC payments are least likely to be in more than one supplemental arrangement among those with employed mothers or with mothers in education and training programs (22 percent). Family size strongly influences the degree to which preschool-age and school-age children are cared for by multiple providers when their mother is employed or in an education or training program. In this case, as the number of children under age 13 in the family increases, the likelihood of having multiple supplemental arrangements decreases (table 3.5). This pattern is most striking for children with employed mothers or with mothers in education and training programs.

Type of Main Arrangement

If parents report that they are the main caregivers, children are less likely to be in more than one supplemental arrangement, regardless of the age of the child or maternal employment status (table 3.5). Also, when parents are reported to be the main providers, few children of nonemployed mothers *not* in education or training programs use more than one regular supplemental arrangement (about 4 percent of either preschool-age or school-age children). Nevertheless, a substantial proportion of children in supplemental main arrangements require the services of more than one caregiver. For children under age 5 whose mothers are employed, this is especially the case for those primarily cared for by a relative (typically a grandparent) or in a center-based program.

Note, chapter 3

1. Interviewers were instructed to collect information on arrangements that occurred at least once a week for the two weeks previous.

Chapter 4

Parental Expenditures on Child Care

This chapter focuses on low-income parents' reports of whether or not they pay for care, whether or not they receive financial assistance for child care, and how much they spend on child care. The share of family budget allocated to child care is calculated. Unlike the previous chapters, the family is used as the unit of analysis. The main survey finds that parental expenditures vary by level of family income. This report focuses on variation among low-income families.

The NCCS provides detailed information on child care expenses for the youngest child and for all children in the family. This survey allows us to characterize who pays, how much they pay up front for child care, and whether or not they receive financial assistance. However, this survey does not provide information on how much of their child care payments may be reimbursed.

Who Pays for Care?

The main survey shows that low-income families are less likely to pay for care than high-income families. Only 42 percent of employed mothers with annual family incomes under $15,000 pay for the care of their youngest preschool-age child, whereas 70 percent of employed mothers with annual family incomes of $50,000 or more pay for such care (Hofferth et al. 1991).

Among low-income families, the likelihood of paying for care varies by characteristics of the youngest child (age and type of main arrangement), household type, maternal employment, poverty status, and AFDC receipt. Though not statistically significant, families are somewhat more likely to pay for the main supplemental arrangement of a child under age 5 (39 percent) than for that of a child aged 5 to 12 (36 percent). Among families with a preschool-age child, those with a youngest child aged 1 to 2 are less likely to pay for care (33 percent) than either those with an infant (45 percent) or those with a youngest child aged 3 to 4 (44 percent; not shown). These percentages are not statistically different from one another. However, families whose youngest child is 10 to 12 years old are significantly less likely to pay for care (17 percent; not shown) than those with a younger child.

Household Type

A smaller proportion of single mothers who are *not* employed pay for the main supplemental arrangement of their youngest child than is the case for other families (table 4.1). For two-parent families and single employed mothers, parents with a child under age 5 are much more likely to pay for care than parents without a preschool-age child. Single mothers who are employed are those most likely to pay for the main supplemental arrangement of their youngest child, especially when they have older children. Among these mothers, nearly 57 percent of those with a child under age 5 and about 48 percent of those whose youngest child is 5 to 12 years old pay for care.

TABLE 4.1

Percentage of Families Paying for Nonparental
Main Arrangement for Youngest Child, by
Household Type and Maternal Employment,
Education, and Training Status

	Youngest Under Age 5		Youngest Ages 5 to 12	
	%	N [a]	%	N [a]
Household Type				
Two parents	44.0	71	26.0	36
Dual employed	56.0	32	26.7	15
One employed	41.0	32	25.5	15
0 employed	*[b]	7	*b	6
Single mother	38.4	180	39.3	185
Employed	56.9	81	47.5	123
Nonemployed	23.2	99	22.8	14
Maternal Employment				
Employed mother	56.7	122	44.4	147
Full-time	65.2	75	46.3	83
Part-time	45.1	40	40.8	53
Nonemployed mother	24.0	128	22.6	74
Education and training	25.7	41	43.6	16
Other	23.2	87	16.6	57
All families	39.2	275	36.4	240

Source: NCCS 1990—Low-Income Study.
Note: Totals for employed mothers include those with unknown hours worked per week.
a. The base or denominator on which these percentages were calculated.
b. Asterisk (*) denotes fewer than 10 cases.

Maternal Employment, Education, and Training Status

Nonemployed mothers participating in education or training programs are as likely to pay for care as employed mothers if their youngest child is of school age (table 4.1). The pattern is different among mothers with a child under age 5. In this case, nonemployed mothers in education and training programs are more similar to other nonemployed mothers— about a quarter of both types of these mothers pay for care. Full-time employed mothers are those most likely to pay for care. For example, 65 percent of full-time employed mothers and 45 percent of part-time employed mothers with a child under age 5 pay for the main supplemental arrangement of their youngest child.

In looking at differences by poverty status, AFDC receipt, and main arrangement, we combined nonemployed mothers enrolled in education or training programs with employed mothers because of the similarities in their use of supplemental care.

Poverty Status and AFDC Receipt

Among families with a child under age 5, employed mothers and mothers in education and training programs are less likely to pay for child care if they are living in poverty than are their above-poverty-level, low-income counterparts (table 4.2). This pattern does not hold among nonemployed mothers *not* in education and training programs nor among mothers whose youngest child is 5 to 12 years old. For example, among those with a youngest child aged 5 to 12, 51 percent of mothers in poverty who are employed or are in education/training pay for care, whereas only 40 percent of their above-poverty counterparts pay for care. Some low-income parents above poverty are reimbursed for their child care expenses, but a large proportion of employed mothers in poverty pay, at least up front, for the main supplemental arrangement of their youngest child.

Mothers who at the time of the survey were AFDC recipients or who received AFDC payments during the year previous were less likely than non-AFDC mothers to be paying for the main supplemental arrangement of their youngest child (table 4.2). This relationship holds whether or not the mother is "em-

TABLE 4.2

Percentage of Families Paying for Nonparental Main Arrangement for Youngest Child, by Poverty Status, AFDC Receipt, and Type of Arrangement

	Youngest Under Age 5				Youngest Ages 5 to 12			
	"Employed" Mother[a]		Nonemployed Mother		"Employed" Mother[a]		Nonemployed Mother	
	%	N[b]	%	N[b]	%	N[b]	%	N[b]
Poverty Status								
Poor	41.6	105	20.8	61	50.5	85	10.4	35
Near poor	56.8	24	16.2	12	52.9	39	9.8	12
Not poor	66.6	33	*c	8	39.9	35	*c	6
AFDC[d] Receipt								
Current or past year	34.5	73	20.5	60	35.1	43	7.8	37
Not AFDC	60.3	91	29.9	26	47.6	120	33.3	20
Main Arrangement								
Relative	25.9	60	8.1	48	25.4	85	2.4	28
In-Home	*c	2	*c	6	82.3	11	*c	4
FDC[e]	86.5	35	*c	6	91.9	24	*c	2
Center	52.9	58	29.1	19	57.9	22	*c	6
Other	*c	8	*c	8	33.0	22	36.7	17
Total	48.9	164	23.2	87	44.3	163	16.6	57

Source: NCCS 1990—Low-Income Study.
a. "Employed" mothers includes those in education and training programs.
b. The base or denominator on which these percentages were calculated.
c. Asterisk (*) denotes fewer than 10 cases.
d. AFDC, Aid to Families with Dependent Children.
e. FDC, family day care.

ployed" and for families with or without a child under age 5. AFDC mothers who are not employed and not in education/ training, and with a youngest child of school age, are least likely to pay for child care (8 percent). Non-AFDC mothers who are employed or in education/training, and with a child under age 5, are most likely to pay for child care (60 percent).

Type of Arrangement

Although small sample sizes limited our analysis by type of arrangement, the findings suggest that parents are less likely to pay for relative care than for nonrelative care, regardless of employment status or age of youngest child (table 4.2). However, about a quarter of employed mothers pay for care provided by a relative, regardless of the age of the youngest child. Few nonemployed mothers pay for relative care, although they do pay for other, nonrelative care. It also appears that center care is heavily subsidized for low-income parents, because only half of all employed mothers or mothers in education/training and one-third of other nonemployed mothers report paying for center-based care.

Financial Assistance with Child Care Expenditures

Assistance in paying for child care comes in a variety of forms. Child care expenses may be paid directly by a government agency in several ways. Examples include contracts with providers for spaces for low-income children and the use of vouchers with which parents pay their providers. In both cases, providers collect their fees directly from the subsidizing agency. Parents may also pay their child care provider themselves and be reimbursed for those expenditures. For example, payments for child care (up to a certain level) are not counted as income in calculating benefits for AFDC recipients. Parents may be reimbursed for part of their child care expenditures through the Child and Dependent Care Tax Credit. Parents may also receive direct payments or credits for child care expenses from private sources. Finally, parents whose children are enrolled in Head Start effectively receive a subsidy for care, since they are not charged for this program, though our data suggest that they do not report this as financial assistance in the same way they report other types of assistance.

Although middle- to higher-income families benefit more from the Child and Dependent Care Tax Credit under the federal income tax system, low-income families are more likely to pay directly or to be reimbursed for their child care expenses (Hofferth et al. 1991). For example, 37 percent of families with annual incomes of $50,000 or more (high-income) and 22 percent of families with annual incomes below $15,000 (low-income) claimed the federal income tax credit in 1988. On the other hand, only 1 percent of high-income families reported receiving any financial assistance for the child care expenses of their youngest child, whereas 13 percent of all low-income families with a child under age 13 reported that they received such assistance.

This section focuses on what type of low-income families are more likely to receive subsidies for care. Respondents were asked whether or not they received any financial help with their child care expenses. In addition, for families with a youngest child enrolled in Head Start, we counted enrollment as a form of subsidization, even if these parents reported no financial help.

Among low-income parents relying on *supplemental care* on a regular basis, 28 percent of families with a child under age 5 and 15 percent of those with the youngest child aged 5 to 12 reported that they receive any financial assistance for their youngest child's care expenses.

Household Type

Dual-employed couples are least likely to report receiving financial assistance for their youngest child's supplemental arrangement—about 8 percent of those with a child under age 5 and 3 percent of those with the youngest child aged 5 to 12 receive aid (not shown). Nonemployed single mothers are more likely to report receiving financial assistance than single mothers who are employed, regardless of the age of the child. Among single mothers with a child under age 5, 19 percent of employed mothers and 44 percent of all nonemployed mothers reported receiving assistance (not shown). Nonemployed single mothers are more likely to be eligible for subsidies because of their lower family incomes.

Maternal Employment, Education, and Training Status

Even when participation in education and training programs is taken into account, nonemployed mothers reported that they are more likely than either full-time or part-time mothers to receive financial assistance for their youngest child's care expenditures. For example, among low-income families with a child under age 5, 64 percent of mothers in education and training programs, 30 percent of other nonemployed mothers, 18 percent of full-time employed mothers, and 10 percent of part-time employed mothers receive financial assistance (not shown).

Poverty Status and AFDC Receipt

A higher proportion of employed mothers in poverty reported receiving financial assistance for their youngest child's supplemental arrangement than other low-income employed mothers, regardless of the age of the youngest child (table 4.3). Among nonemployed mothers, however, those living near poverty (i.e., between 100 percent and 125 percent of the poverty line) are more likely to receive financial assistance than those living in poverty or those living above 125 percent of the poverty level.

Mothers currently receiving AFDC are much more likely to report receiving financial assistance for their youngest child's supplemental care than mothers not currently receiving AFDC payments, regardless of the age of the youngest child or employment status of the mother (table 4.3). In particular, employed mothers currently on AFDC with a child under age 5 are most likely to report receiving financial assistance (67 percent).

Source of Assistance

Low-income parents reported that the government provides most of the financial assistance to help families with their child care expenses: 86 percent of families who reported receiving aid get that aid from the government (figure 4.1). Employers, on the other hand, play a very minor role in subsidizing the care of children from low-income families. Only 1 percent of low-income families receiving assistance get help from employers; a higher proportion of low-income families (9 percent) depend on the financial assistance of friends and relatives.

Type of Arrangement

The degree to which parents receive financial assistance depends most strongly on the type of main supplemental arrangement used by the youngest child in the family (figure 4.2). Families using center care as the main arrangement for the youngest child are much more likely to report receiving financial assistance (43 percent) than those relying on family day care homes (6 percent) or relatives (5 percent). Among those receiving assistance, the government is the main source of assistance for families using either center care or relative care: 93 percent of parents receiving financial assistance with center care (including Head Start) and 84 percent of those receiving financial assistance with care provided by a relative get that help from the government (figure 4.3).

TABLE 4.3

Percentage of Families Receiving Any Direct Financial Assistance for Care of their Youngest Child (Those Using Nonparental Care)

| | Youngest Under Age 5 | | | | Youngest Ages 5 to 12 | | | |
| | "Employed" Mother[a] | | Nonemployed Mother | | "Employed" Mother[a] | | Nonemployed Mother | |
	%	N[b]	%	N[b]	%	N[b]	%	N[b]
Poverty Status								
Poor	34.3	118	28.3	85	16.0	100	16.5	44
Near poor	19.1	32	46.4	14	7.2	47	25.5	13
Not poor	12.7	37	18.6	11	3.7	47	*[c]	8
AFDC[d] Receipt								
Current year	67.2	14	38.5	21	44.9	10	*[c]	8
Past year	41.4	70	31.1	54	21.7	42	29.6	38
Not AFDC	12.8	105	24.0	42	5.2	146	4.3	24
Total	27.4	189	29.7	117	10.7	198	18.3	69

Source: NCCS 1990—Low-Income Study.
a. "Employed" mothers includes those in education and training programs.
b. The base or denominator on which these percentages were calculated.
c. Asterisk (*) denotes fewer than 10 cases.
d. AFDC, Aid to Families with Dependent Children.

FIGURE 4.1

Source of Assistance for Nonparental Main Arrangement for Youngest Child

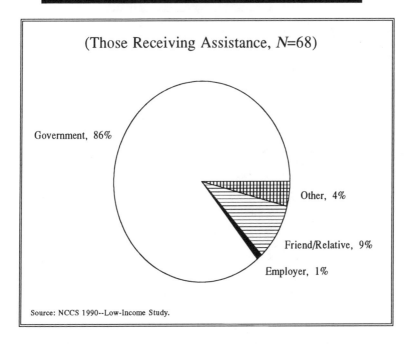

(Those Receiving Assistance, *N*=68)

Government, 86%

Other, 4%

Friend/Relative, 9%

Employer, 1%

Source: NCCS 1990--Low-Income Study.

Mean Expenditures and Budget Shares

The main survey finds that, among families who pay for care, low-income parents spend a far greater share of their weekly family income on child care than high-income parents. For example, the main survey reports that, among families with a preschool-age child, employed mothers with annual family incomes of $50,000 or more pay an average of $85 a week for the care of all the children in the family, or 6 percent of their family income, on average. However, employed mothers with an annual family income under $15,000 pay an

FIGURE 4.2

Percentage of Families Receiving Direct Financial
Assistance for Youngest Child, by Type of Care

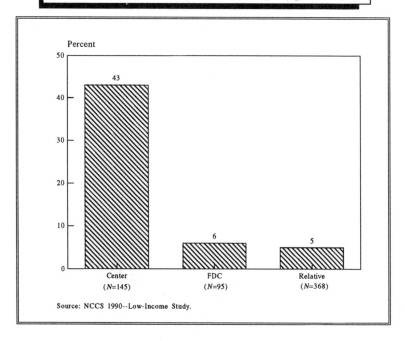

Source: NCCS 1990--Low-Income Study.

average of $38 per week, or about 25 percent of their family income on average (Hofferth et al. 1991).

Child care is a major part of the family budget, comparable to food and housing. Across families of all incomes, food typically accounts for 13 percent of all family expenditures, and housing accounts for 27 percent of all family expenditures (U.S. Bureau of the Census 1989). The *relative* expenditures on care are much higher for low-income families. This section examines differences among low-income families in the proportion of income spent on child care.

Without controlling for employment status, low-income families who pay for the care of a child under age 5 (i.e., 49 percent) spend an average of $36 a week for the care of all

FIGURE 4.3

Percentage of Families Receiving Direct Assistance
from the Government for Youngest Child, by Type
of Care (Those Receiving Assistance Only)

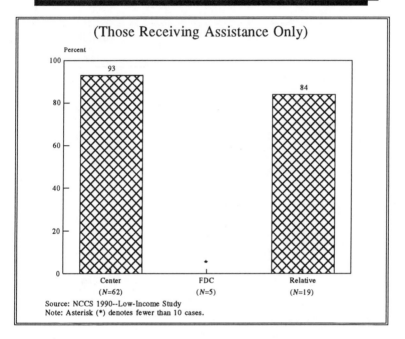

(Those Receiving Assistance Only)

Source: NCCS 1990--Low-Income Study
Note: Asterisk (*) denotes fewer than 10 cases.

children in the family (table 4.4). This represents an average
of 23 percent of their weekly gross family income. Low-income families whose youngest child is of school age spend
somewhat less—an average of $30 a week and an average of
19 percent of their total weekly income. Both the *absolute*
level of expenditures and the *relative* level of expenditures
on child care vary among low-income families by other key
characteristics of the family.

Household Type

Single mothers spend more per week than two-parent families
in absolute and relative terms. Moreover, among those with

TABLE 4.4

Mean Total Weekly Expenditure and Budget Share by Poverty Status and AFDC Receipt (Families Paying for Care)

	Youngest Under Age 5			Youngest Ages 5 to 12		
	$	% Income	N[a]	$	% Income	N[a]
Poverty Status						
Poor	33.7	27.2	59	25.0	24.3	34
Near poor	39.9	19.5	17	35.3	17.1	23
Not poor	37.8	15.7	27	30.7	12.1	23
AFDC Receipt						
Current or past year	30.4	25.3	38	29.6	31.4	17
Not AFDC[b]	39.0	21.5	65	29.6	15.2	63
Total	35.8	22.9	103	29.6	18.7	80

Source: NCCS 1990—Low-Income Study.
a. The total number of families in this category.
b. AFDC, Aid to Families with Dependent Children.

a child under age 5, dual-employed couples spend about the *same amount* of money on child care as employed single mothers on average ($37 versus $39 per week; not shown). Yet employed single mothers spend a much *greater share* of their family budget on child care than dual-employed couples (28 percent versus 17 percent; not shown).

A similar pattern exists for two-parent families with only one working parent, and for nonemployed single mothers. Two parents with one wage earner spend $27 per week, or 14 percent of their family budget (not shown). Nonemployed single mothers spend $31 per week, or 26 percent of their family budget. Because of sample size limitations, we could not evaluate average expenditures and budget shares by household type for families with older children.

Maternal Employment, Education, and Training Status

Full-time employed mothers spend a greater *absolute* amount on total child care expenses than other mothers, regardless of the age of the youngest child (figure 4.4). Part-time employed mothers with a child under age 5, however, carry a heavier financial burden in that they spend a greater *proportion* of their total family income (27 percent) on child care than other low-income mothers (figure 4.5). Among all low-income families with a child under age 5, mothers in education and training programs spend about $23 a week on child care for about 15 percent of their family budget (figures 4.4 and 4.5); these averages are lower than those of other low-income mothers with a child under age 5. The latter are less likely to pay for care in the first place.

Poverty Status and AFDC Receipt

The standard of living and participation in the AFDC program also influence low-income families' expenditures on child care. Although families in poverty spend fewer dollars than other low-income families on average, families in poverty spend a substantially greater proportion of their family resources on the care of their children, regardless of the age of the youngest child (table 4.4). At the same time, AFDC families spend a higher proportion of their total family income on child care than low-income families who have not been on AFDC in the past year, especially among families whose youngest child is of school age (table 4.4). Clearly, one must consider not only the *absolute* expenditures on child care but also the *relative* expenditures on such care.

FIGURE 4.4

Mean Total Week Expenditure for All Children in Family, by Maternal Employment, Educatio, and Training, and Age of Child (Families Paying for Care)

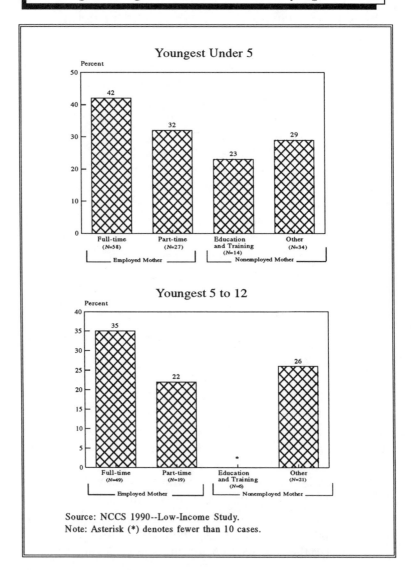

Source: NCCS 1990--Low-Income Study.
Note: Asterisk (*) denotes fewer than 10 cases.

FIGURE 4.5

Mean Percentage of Family Income Spent on Child Care by Maternal Employment, Education, and Training, and Age of Child (Families Paying for Care)

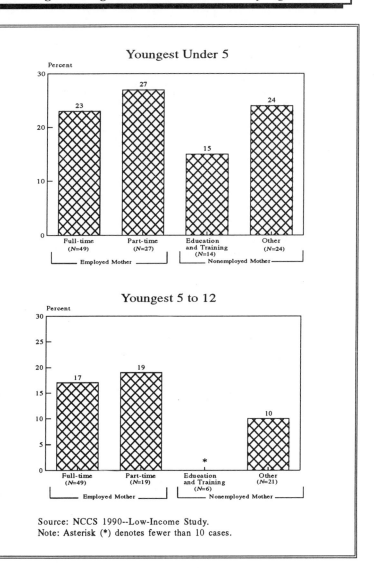

Source: NCCS 1990--Low-Income Study.
Note: Asterisk (*) denotes fewer than 10 cases.

Chapter Five

Parental Preference

This chapter explores parental satisfaction with current care and preferences for alternative care arrangements. Although many researchers have inferred preference from current patterns of arrangements, the current arrangements used by parents may not be accurate indicators of parental preference. Drawing conclusions from survey questions about levels of satisfaction is also problematic because parents consistently report high levels of satisfaction with current arrangements across numerous surveys. Parents may report that they are highly satisfied because they *are* satisfied. High levels of satisfaction may also be a function of the questionnaire wording and response categories, as well as a rationalization of parents' choices (Sonenstein 1991). Given this problem of interpretation, the desire to change arrangements may be a better indicator of parental preference. However, one should keep in mind that responses to hypothetical questions are only that; the choices parents would make given a different set of options and constraints cannot be determined. Although the desire to change arrangements may not predict parental preferences and choices under different conditions, it still may be a more accurate indicator of parents' current preferences than indicators used in the past.

Parental Satisfaction with Current Arrangements

We focus here on families with children under age 5 because the NCCS did not ask all families whose youngest child is of school age about their level of satisfaction with current arrangements or about their desire to change arrangements. If respondents designated "school" or "lessons" as the arrangement used for the greatest number of hours per week for their youngest child, they were not asked these questions. Therefore the sample of low-income families with school-age children was too small for reliable estimates of parental preferences, and we focused, instead, on families with preschool-age children.

Parents were asked how satisfied they were with the main arrangement for their youngest child. The response categories were "highly satisfied," "satisfied," "not completely satisfied," and "dissatisfied." Few parents who rely on any supplemental care reported that they were not satisfied with the current main arrangement for their youngest child under age 5: about 95 percent were satisfied or highly satisfied. Two-parent families were more highly satisfied than single mothers: 84 percent of two-parent families and 67 percent of single mothers were highly satisfied with the current main arrangement of their youngest child under age 5 (not shown). However, overall satisfaction did not significantly vary by parental employment status.

Among low-income families with a child under age 5, parents were most highly satisfied with the youngest child's main arrangement if that child was cared for by a parent (77 percent) or relative (81 percent; not shown). Low-income parents of preschool-age children were least satisfied with center care, although they are still quite satisfied in general (60 percent are highly satisfied; not shown). Nevertheless, there was no significant difference in satisfaction between parents solely relying on themselves as caregivers and families using some supplemental care (not shown).

Desire to Change Current Arrangements

Although few parents reported dissatisfaction with their current arrangements, some parents would like to change their current combination of arrangements. Respondents were asked: "Assuming you could have any type or combination of care arrangements you wanted for your youngest child, would you prefer some other type or combination of types instead of what you have now?" Approximately 27 percent of low-income parents with a child under age 5 wanted to change arrangements. Among parents reporting a desire to change current arrangements, most would prefer center care (68 percent; not shown). Nevertheless, the degree to which parents want a different arrangement of any type varies by other characteristics of the family.

Household Type

Single mothers are significantly more likely to want to change their youngest child's current arrangements than two-parent families (35 percent versus 16 percent, respectively; not shown). In particular, employed single mothers are most likely to want to change arrangements (43 percent), compared to other household types (figure 5.1). Single mothers who are not employed are similar to dual-employed parents in the degree to which they desire different arrangements (30 percent and 26 percent, respectively).

Maternal Employment, Education, and Training Status

Employed mothers are somewhat more likely than nonemployed mothers to desire alternative arrangements (34 percent versus 23 percent, respectively; not shown). In fact, nonemployed mothers in education and training programs are least likely to want to change arrangements (17 percent; figure 5.2).

FIGURE 5.1

Percentage of Parents Who Want to Change
Current Combination of Care, by Household
Type (Youngest Child Under Age 5)

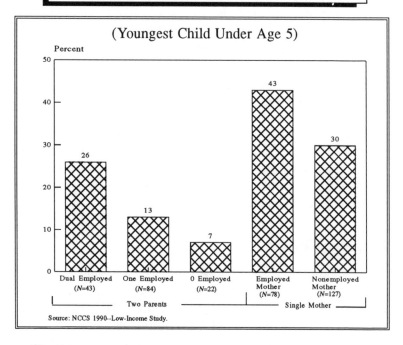

(Youngest Child Under Age 5)

Source: NCCS 1990--Low-Income Study.

AFDC Receipt and Other Financial Factors

There is no distinct pattern according to AFDC receipt or
poverty status, but families receiving financial assistance for
the youngest child's main arrangement are somewhat less
likely to prefer a different combination of care than families
not receiving financial assistance (15 percent versus 29 percent, respectively; not shown). Furthermore, families who
pay for the main supplemental arrangement of their youngest
child are also more likely to want alternative arrangements
than those who do not pay for such care—32 percent versus
26 percent, respectively, among those with a child under age

FIGURE 5.2

Percentage of Parents Who Want to Change Current Combination of Care by Maternal Employment, Education, and Training

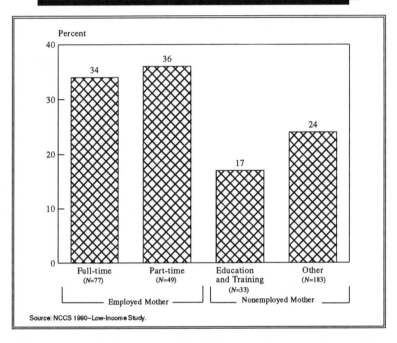

Source: NCCS 1990–Low-Income Study.

5 (not shown). However, this difference between those who pay and do not pay is not statistically significant.

Type of Arrangement

Figure 5.3 details the proportion of parents who desire a different combination of care by the type of main arrangement for their youngest child under age 5. Families relying on center care as the main arrangement are less likely to want to change their combination of care arrangements (19 percent) than other families with a child under age 5. Families currently relying on relatives as their main arrangement are most likely to want to change arrangements (36 percent).

FIGURE 5.3

Percentage of Parents Who Want to Change Current
Combination of Care, by Type of Main Arrangement
for Youngest Child (Youngest Child Under Age 5)

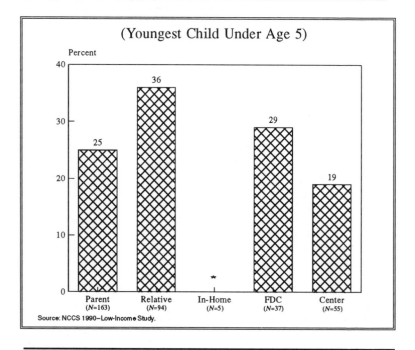

(Youngest Child Under Age 5)

Source: NCCS 1990–Low-Income Study.

Reasons for Preferring an Alternative Arrangement

When asked why they would prefer an alternative arrangement, a majority (70 percent) of low-income parents with a
child under age 5 cited quality of care as the major reason
(figure 5.4). Quality was cited slightly more often by low-income parents than by parents of all income levels; the main
survey reports that 60 percent of all parents in the United
States who preferred an alternative arrangement said quality

FIGURE 5.4

Why Prefer an Alternative Arrangement?
Families with Youngest Child Under Age 5

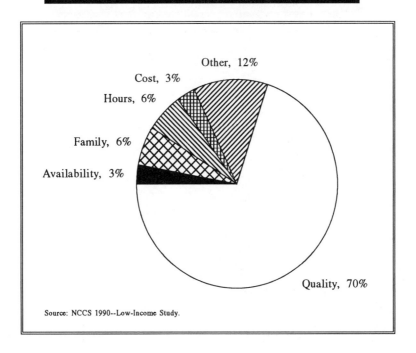

Other, 12%

Cost, 3%

Hours, 6%

Family, 6%

Availability, 3%

Quality, 70%

Source: NCCS 1990--Low-Income Study.

was the reason (Hofferth et al. 1991). Child care expenditures play a relatively minor role in parents' reasons for preferring alternative arrangements. Only 3 percent of low-income parents with a child under age 5 want to change arrangements because of "cost" (figure 5.4). This is particularly noteworthy for low-income families, since those families who pay tend to spend a much greater share of their income on child care.

Because the absolute number of parents who desire an alternative arrangement is small among this sample of low-income families with a child under age 5, we could not classify the reasons for preferring an alternative arrangement by the type of arrangement desired by the parents. However,

FIGURE 5.5

Most Important Aspect of Quality in
Preference for Alternative Arrangement
(Youngest Child Under Age 5)

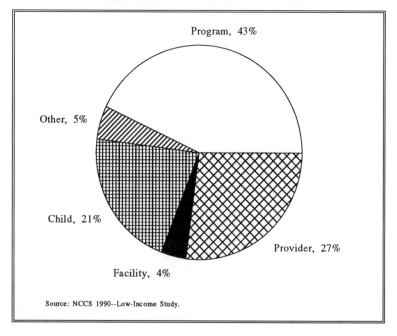

Source: NCCS 1990--Low-Income Study.

when we looked at the arrangement most often preferred by
parents (i.e., center-based care), we found that 78 percent of
parents who prefer centers cite "quality" as the most important reason (not shown).

Among those who cited quality as the major reason for
wanting an alternative arrangement, low-income parents with
a child under age 5 reported that program characteristics (e.g.,
school preparation, development, religious, or cultural in-
struction) are the most important aspects of quality (43 percent;
figure 5.5). In fact, child development and school preparation
were cited most often (20 percent and 19 percent, respectively; not shown). Figure 5.5 also shows that 27 percent of

parents stated that characteristics of the child care provider (e.g., personal style, training, reliability) were the most important aspects of quality in preferring an alternative arrangement, and 21 percent referred to child-related factors (e.g., age range) as the most important aspects. These findings support evidence based on families of all income levels from the main survey: 39 percent cited program characteristics, 26 percent cited provider characteristics, and 20 percent cited child-related factors (Hofferth et al. 1991).

Chapter Six

Summary

This report has examined the care arrangements of children under age 13 in families with annual incomes below $15,000. We investigated (1) how low-income children are regularly cared for, (2) how much low-income families spend on child care, and (3) what kind of arrangements low-income parents prefer. Our findings are based on data from the National Child Care Survey, 1990, and its supplemental sample of low-income households. The complete low-income sample consisted of 973 families, with a total of 1,751 children under age 13. Thus, this study represents approximately 6.6 million households with annual incomes below $15,000 and a child under age 13, and the 12 million children under age 13 in these families.

Care Arrangements among Low-Income Children

Although parents are the principal source of child care in low-income families in the United States, over two-thirds of low-income children under age 13 are cared for by someone other than a parent on a regular weekly basis. About 38 percent of children under age 5 and 33 percent of children aged 5 to 12 are cared for solely by their parents. The proportion of low-income children in exclusive parental care depends on family structure and parental employment status. Children in two-parent families are substantially more likely than children of single mothers to be cared for exclusively by their parents. Moreover, nonemployed parents are more likely than employed parents to provide exclusive parental care for their children, regardless of family structure.

When we examined the arrangements in which low-income children spend the greatest amount of time each week, we confirmed that supplemental arrangements play an important part in the lives of low-income children. Approximately 58 percent of both preschool-age and school-age children have at least one supplemental arrangement. Children under age 5 are just as likely to be in the care of another relative (22 percent) as to be in the care of a nonrelative (25 percent) as their *main* arrangement each week. Nearly 20 percent of school-age children are primarily cared for by another relative, whereas 14 percent are in the care of an unrelated provider as their *main* arrangement. About 17 percent of children under age 5 and 11 percent of children aged 5 to 12 are primarily cared for by a grandparent.

This report also examined the extent to which parents rely on any care *at all* by a grandparent on a regular weekly basis, that is, at least once a week for the two weeks previous, *regardless of the relative amount of time*. Grandparents play a predominant role in caring for low-income children, especially for children of single mothers and children in two-parent families where both parents are employed. For example, 35 percent of preschool-age children of single mothers and 35 percent of preschool-age children in dual-employed families are in the care of a grandparent for some period of time on a regular weekly basis.

By disaggregating care types of nonrelative supplemental care, we found that only a small proportion of low-income children are cared for by a nonrelative in the child's own home, whereas a higher proportion use family day care providers and centers for some period of time each week. Only 2 percent of low-income children under age 5 are cared for by a nonrelative in the child's home, 8 percent are cared for by a nonrelative in another private home (family day care), and just under 15 percent are in center-based programs (including Head Start) as their main arrangement. In particular, children under age 5 are more likely to be enrolled in family day care or in center-based care if the family is headed by a single employed mother than children in other low-income families. Moreover, children under age 5 whose mothers are not employed but are in education and training programs are more likely to be in center-based care (35 percent) than any other type of main arrangement.

These percentages increased when we examined the degree to which nonrelative care is used at all, not simply as the *main* arrangement. Approximately 6 percent of preschool-age and school-age children in low-income families are in the care of an unrelated provider in the child's home for some period of time each week. Among low-income children under age 5, 20 percent use centers and 12 percent use family day care providers at *all*. Among low-income children aged 5 to 12, 11 percent are in a center-based program and 6 percent are cared for by a nonrelative in another private home at *all*. Although only 11 percent of low-income children aged 5 to 12 participate in after-school activities such as lessons, sports, and clubs as their main arrangement, 30 percent participate in these activities on a regular basis for some period of time.

Head Start enrollments vary significantly by parental employment, race, and poverty status, but not by family structure. Children with nonemployed parents and children in poverty are more likely to be enrolled in Head Start than other low-income children. Moreover, children with nonemployed mothers in education or training programs are most likely to be in a Head Start program (30 percent), while children of employed mothers are least likely to be in a Head Start program (6 percent of those with part-time employed mothers and 8 percent of those with full-time employed mothers). We estimate that in 1990, only 29 percent of 4-year-olds in poverty were in a Head Start program.

Child care consists of a combination of arrangements for many families; many children use more than one supplemental arrangement each week. For example, children may be in a center-based program and may also be cared for by a relative, in addition to being cared for by their parents. About 24 percent of low-income children under age 5 and 28 percent of low-income children aged 5 to 12 are in more than one supplemental arrangement on a regular weekly basis. Children of single mothers are substantially more likely than children in two-parent families to use more than one supplemental arrangement, regardless of the age of the child. Among children under age 5, 31 percent of those with single mothers and 14 percent of those in two-parent families are in more than one supplemental arrangement. Moreover, a substantial proportion of children of single mothers who are *not* employed use more than one supplemental arrangement on a regular basis— 24 percent of both preschool-age children and school-age children. Also, children of full-time employed mothers are more likely than children of part-time employed mothers to use more than one supplemental arrangement (44 percent versus 27 percent among children under age 5, respectively).

Overall, one of the most important findings of this report is that the child care arrangements used by children with employed mothers are quite similar to those used by children with nonemployed mothers enrolled in education or training programs. When the child care arrangements of nonemployed mothers are examined without regard to other employment-enhancing activities, we found that nonemployed mothers as a group have a different pattern of arrangements than employed mothers. However, the child care demands of education and training programs are similar to the child care demands of employment.

Time Spent in Supplemental Care

The amount of time that low-income children spend in a supplemental main arrangement depends on the age of the child as well as on family structure and parental employment status. Low-income children under age 5 in supplemental care spend an average of 28 hours per week in their main supplemental arrangement, and children aged 5 to 12 spend an average of 13 hours per week in this supplemental arrangement. Young children in families headed by a single mother spend more time in a supplemental main arrangement than children in two-parent families (29 hours versus 22 hours per week, respectively). Preschool-age children of single mothers who are employed typically spend the greatest amount of time in a supplemental main arrangement each week (38 hours). The number of hours in supplemental care as a main arrangement does not vary significantly by poverty status or AFDC receipt, after maternal employment status is taken into account.

Parental Expenditures on Child Care

The NCCS shows that low-income families are less likely to pay for child care than high-income families; among employed mothers with a child under age 5, 42 percent with annual family incomes below $15,000, and 70 percent with annual family incomes of $50,000 or more pay for care (Hofferth et al. 1991). Nevertheless, the likelihood of paying for care varies by key characteristics *among* low-income families. Single mothers who are employed are those most likely to pay for the supplemental main arrangement of their youngest child, especially when they have younger children. Among these mothers, nearly 57 percent of those with a child under age 5 and about 48 percent of those whose youngest child is of school age pay for care. Overall, families in poverty or receiving AFDC payments are less likely to pay for care than other low-income families.

Among low-income parents relying on any supplemental child care on a regular basis, only 27 percent of families with a preschool-age child and 15 percent of those with the youngest child aged 5 to 12 reported receiving any financial assistance for their youngest child's care arrangements. A higher proportion of both employed mothers in poverty and mothers currently receiving AFDC payments reported receiving financial assistance than did other low-income employed mothers. In particular, employed mothers currently on AFDC with a child under age 5 were most likely to report receiving financial assistance (67 percent).

The government provides most of the financial assistance reported by low-income families: 86 percent of low-income families who reported receiving assistance receive it from the government. Only 1 percent of low-income families receiving assistance get help from employers; a higher proportion (9 percent) of low-income families rely on the financial assistance of friends and relatives.

Although low-income families are less likely to pay for care and spend fewer dollars on care than high-income families, they spend a substantially greater share of their income on the care of their children. Moreover, families in poverty spend an even higher proportion of their family budget on child care than other low-income families. For example, among low-income families with a child under age 5, those in poverty spend an average of $33 each week—representing 27 percent of their family income—whereas those living at 125 percent above the federal poverty line spend an average of $38 each week, representing 16 percent of their family income. In contrast, employed mothers with annual family incomes of $50,000 or more pay an average of $85 a week, or 6 percent of their family income on average (Hofferth et al. 1991).

Parental Preference

This report also explored parental satisfaction with current care and preferences for alternative care arrangements among families with annual incomes below $15,000 and with a child under age 5. We found that about 95 percent of low-income families with a child under age 5 are satisfied or highly satisfied with the current main arrangement for their youngest child. Moreover, low-income parents relying on some form of supplemental care reported that they are just as satisfied with their current arrangements as low-income parents caring exclusively for their children.

Although almost all low-income parents with a child under age 5 reported that they are satisfied, 27 percent want to change their current type or combination of child care arrangements. There is no distinct pattern in preferences according to AFDC receipt or poverty status, but single mothers are significantly more likely to want to change their youngest preschool-age child's current arrangements (35 percent) than two-parent families (16 percent). Among parents reporting a desire to change arrangements, 68 percent would prefer center-based care. Moreover, families relying on center care as the main arrangement for their youngest child under age 5 are less likely to want to change arrangements (19 percent) than are those relying on relatives as the main arrangement (36 percent).

When asked why they would prefer an alternative arrangement, 70 percent of low-income parents with a child under age 5 cited quality as the most important reason. Whe.eas low-income families spend a relatively larger proportion of their family income on child care, only 3 percent of low-income parents with a child under age 5 said they wanted to change arrangements because of "cost." Finally, those who cited quality as the major reason for wanting an alternative arrangement most often reported that characteristics of the program, not the provider, are the most important aspects of quality.

In making their decisions about child care and employment, low-income parents make complicated trade-offs between location, cost, convenience, quality, and preference for someone they know and are comfortable with. This study shows that child care arrangements, expenditures, and parental preferences among low-income families vary according to characteristics of the child and the family.

APPENDICES

Appendix A

Design Effects for Survey Percentages

The two tables in this appendix provide generalized 95 percent confidence limits for survey percentages for the two different units of analysis in this report: (1) low-income children under age 13 and (2) low-income families with a youngest child under age 13. The 95 percent confidence limits apply to all sample children and families, as well as to subclasses of children and families.

To construct these tables, Abt Associates computed standard errors for both types of samples using nine survey variables. The selected variables include main child care arrangement and demographic and socioeconomic status characteristics. An average design effect was derived for both children and families. The design effect equals the ratio of the cluster sampling variance to the sample variance yielded by a simple random sample.

TABLE A.1

Confidence Limits for All Low-Income Children Under Age 13

Sample Size	Average Design Effect	95% Confidence Limits (%)					
		5, or 95%	10, or 90%	20, or 80%	30, or 70%	40, or 60%	50%
1,753	2.80	1.7	2.3	3.1	3.6	3.8	3.9
1,652	2.69	1.7	2.4	3.2	3.6	3.9	4.0
1,600	2.63	1.7	2.4	3.2	3.6	3.9	4.0
1,500	2.52	1.8	2.4	3.2	3.7	3.9	4.0
1,400	2.41	1.8	2.4	3.3	3.7	4.0	4.1
1,300	2.31	1.8	2.5	3.3	3.8	4.0	4.1
1,200	2.20	1.8	2.5	3.4	3.8	4.1	4.2
1,100	2.09	1.9	2.6	3.4	3.9	4.2	4.3
1,000	1.98	1.9	2.6	3.5	4.0	4.3	4.4
900	1.87	1.9	2.7	3.6	4.1	4.4	4.5
800	1.76	2.0	2.8	3.7	4.2	4.5	4.6
700	1.66	2.1	2.9	3.8	4.4	4.7	4.8
600	1.55	2.2	3.0	4.0	4.6	4.9	5.0
500	1.44	2.3	3.2	4.2	4.8	5.2	5.3
400	1.33	2.5	3.4	4.5	5.2	5.5	5.7
300	1.22	2.7	3.8	5.0	5.7	6.1	6.3
200	1.11	3.2	4.4	5.9	6.7	7.2	7.3
100	1.01	4.3	5.9	7.9	9.0	9.6	9.8
50	1.00	6.0	8.3	11.1	12.7	13.6	13.9

Note: For a given sample size, the chances are 95 in 100 that the actual population percentage lies in the range formed by the sample percentage minus the number given in the table and the sample percentage plus the number given in the table.

TABLE A.2

Confidence Limits for Low-Income Families with Youngest Child Under Age 13

Sample Size	Average Design Effect	95% Confidence Limits (%)					
		5, or 95%	10, or 90%	20, or 80%	30, or 70%	40, or 60%	50%
973	1.37	1.6	2.2	2.9	3.4	3.6	3.7
900	1.34	1.6	2.3	3.0	3.5	3.7	3.8
800	1.30	1.7	2.4	3.2	3.6	3.9	3.9
700	1.25	1.8	2.5	3.3	3.8	4.1	4.1
600	1.21	1.9	2.6	3.5	4.0	4.3	4.4
500	1.17	2.1	2.8	3.8	4.3	4.6	4.7
400	1.13	2.3	3.1	4.2	4.8	5.1	5.2
300	1.09	2.6	3.5	4.7	5.4	5.8	5.9
200	1.04	3.1	4.2	5.7	6.5	6.9	7.1
100	1.00	4.3	5.9	7.8	9.0	9.6	9.8
50	1.00	6.0	8.3	11.1	12.7	13.6	13.9

Note: For a given sample size, the chances are 95 in 100 that the actual population percentage lies in the range formed by the sample percentage minus the number given in the table and the sample percentage plus the number given in the table.

Appendix B

Sample Distributions and Population Estimates of Low-Income Children Under Age 13

TABLE B.1

Sample Distributions and Population Estimates of Low-Income Children Under Age 13

Key Characteristics	Children Under 5 %	N	Pop. (000)	Children 5 to 12 %	N	Pop. (000)	Total Pop. (000)	N	%
Household Type									
Two parents	43.6	310	2,117	35.6	371	2,536	4,653	680	38.9
Dual employed	10.6	175	514	9.9	103	701	1,216	178	10.2
One employed	24.2	72	1,178	18.9	196	1,344	2,521	369	21.1
0 employed	8.8	62	425	6.9	72	491	916	134	7.7
Single mother	51.6	366	2,505	57.5	599	4,094	6,599	965	55.1
Employed	16.8	119	816	26.4	275	1,879	2,695	394	22.5
Nonemployed	34.8	247	1,689	31.1	324	2,214	3,904	571	32.6
Single father	.6	4	30	2.1	22	149	179	26	1.5
No parents	4.2	30	204	4.7	49	336	541	79	4.5
Maternal Employment									
Employed mother	32.1	217	1,483	44.2	427	2,922	4,404	644	39.2
Full-time	17.0	115	786	24.1	233	1,593	2,379	348	21.2
Part-time	13.0	88	600	16.5	159	1,088	1,688	247	15.0
Nonemployed mother	67.9	458	3,132	55.8	539	3,688	6,819	997	60.8
Education and training	9.4	64	434	6.4	62	423	858	125	7.6
Other	58.4	394	2,697	49.4	477	3,264	5,961	872	53.1
Total	100.0	710	4,614	100.0	1,041	7,115	11,972	1,751	100.0

Source: National Child Care Survey, 1990—Low Income Study.
Notes: Percentages may not sum to 100, and sample frequencies may not sum to total sample size because of rounding and/or missing values.

Glossary of Terms

Aid to Families with Dependent Children (AFDC). A federal welfare program that is administered by the U.S. Department of Health and Human Services to provide funds for low-income, especially female-headed, families with children. Such families may receive subsidized child care.

Categories of Child Care. For this study, we were interested in any type of child care used at least once a week during the two weeks preceding the interview. It did not matter what the parent was doing during this time; all that mattered was regularity. Families use child care for a variety of reasons, including employment, attending school, or engaging in other activities. This report uses the following categories of child care:

Center-Based Programs. Established settings where children are cared for in a group away from their homes for all or part of the day. There are many different kinds of center-based care, including nursery schools, preschools, and parent cooperatives. Some of these centers are set up primarily to provide work-related care, and others are designed to prepare children for their school years. Centers provide care for groups of children ranging in age from infancy through school age.

Family Day Care (FDC). A private home where an adult cares for children from infancy through school age on a regular basis. The care is provided at the home of the caregiver, *not* the child's home. The family day care provider is often a mother who has children of her own for whom she is also caring. Family day care can be licensed or unlicensed. The number of children in a family day care home varies with the situation. If two or more women join together to operate an FDC home, it may be referred to as a group home or minicenter. This report classifies care by someone not related to the child in another private home as FDC. This provider can be a friend, neighbor, or someone that the family did not previously know.

Father Care. Care by the father or husband/partner of the mother on a regular basis when the mother is not at home.

Grandparent Care. Care by a grandmother or grandfather in the child's home or in the grandparent's home.

Head Start. A comprehensive program offering help with educational needs, health, nutrition, and social services for low-income children between the ages of 3 and 5. Head Start is typically a half-day, part-week program that relies heavily on parental involvement.

In-Home Care. Generally a nonrelative who takes care of one family's children in the children's own home. Sometimes a provider brings her own child/ children along to a home. Another common situation is for two families to share an in-home provider.

Lessons, Sports, Clubs. School-age children may participate in a variety of activities after school, varying by day of the week and season of the year. Any activity such as soccer, music lessons, scouts, and so forth should be included in this category.

Self-Care. The child is responsible for his or her own care. Children who are responsible for themselves after school are often referred to as "latchkey kids," since they let themselves into their own homes.

Child Care Expenses. This report examines two measures of parental child care expenditures: mean weekly expenditures for all children under age 13 in the family and mean percentage of family income spent on child care.

Weekly Expenditures. The NCCS contains detailed information on the parental expenditures for the care of the youngest child in the family. For each arrangement of the youngest child, parents could respond in terms of hourly, daily, weekly, monthly, or annual payments. Using the child's time diary of care arrangements, payments were converted to weekly expenditures. For one-child families, the total weekly expenditure is the sum of weekly payments across all arrangements. If there was more than one child under age 13, parents were also asked how much they spent for all the arrangements used by all children under age 13 in the family. For those few parents who listed their expenditures by the hour or day, their total weekly expenditure was estimated according to the age of their youngest child and the average number of hours and days per week spent by all children in the sample under age 5, as well as between ages 5 and 12, in a paid main arrangement. Estimates of weekly expenditures exclude noncash payments and are made only for those families who pay for any child care services.

Budget Shares. For each family in the sample, we have calculated the percentage of their weekly family income that constitutes total weekly child care expenditures for all children. The average proportion of family income spent on child care estimated by the U.S. Bureau of the Census is *not* comparable to our family-based measure. The Census Bureau calculates the mean child care budget share, not on a family-by-family basis, but as the ratio of the sum of weekly expenditures across all families over the sum of weekly income across all families.

Employment Status. Persons in the NCCS are classified as being employed in the week preceding the interview if they either (a) worked as paid employees or worked in their own business or (b) were temporarily absent from their job either with or without pay. Mothers who reported themselves as usually working 35 hours or more each week are classified as *full-time employed*; mothers who report that they usually work fewer than 35 hours each week are classified as *part-time employed*. Mothers who were not employed but listed school or training as their major activity in the week preceding the interview are classified as *nonemployed mothers in education or training programs*. Nonemployed mothers *not* in education or training programs are classified as *other nonemployed mothers.*

Family Income. Total gross annual income from all family members in the year preceding the interview. The income estimates are based on money income alone and do not include noncash benefits.

Household Type. Family structure and parental employment status jointly define household type. Mothers living with a partner or spouse are classified as *two-parent families*. Families headed by a female without a partner or spouse present are classified as *single-mother families*. Within these two types, families are categorized according to the employment status of the parents. Two-parent families consist of *dual employed, one employed,* and *no employed* parents. Single mothers can be either *employed or nonemployed*. Children are also in families headed by a *single father* and in households with *no parents* present.

Poverty Status. Persons whose annual family income fell below the federal poverty threshold are classified as living *in poverty in 1989*. Persons whose family income was 100 percent up to 125 percent of the poverty threshold are classified as living *near poverty*, whereas persons whose family income was 125 percent or more of the poverty threshold are defined as *not poor*. The average poverty threshold for a family of four in 1989 was about $12,675 annually.

Data Quality

Evaluation of Low-Income Data

Our report on the low-income sample (families with annual incomes below $15,000) shows that 29 percent of 4-year-old children in such families who were poor, 23 percent of children in such families whose incomes were within 125 percent of poverty, and 9 percent of children in other families were enrolled in Head Start (figure 3.22). Some people have questioned the large proportion of nonpoor families whose children were said to be enrolled in Head Start. We remind readers that these enrollment rates apply only to children in families with incomes under $15,000, not to all U.S. families. We have tried to emphasize the very restricted nature of the sample on which the current report is based.

However, the question arose as to what percentage of children in all eligible families were enrolled in Head Start in 1990. Consequently, we calculated Head Start enrollments of eligible children based upon all families, not just our low-income sample. These revised figures showed that 29 percent of 4-year-old poor and near-poor children and only 4 percent of 4-year-old children from nonpoor families were enrolled in Head Start (appendix figure D.1). We compared our figures with estimates of the proportion of poor children enrolled in Head Start calculated from Current Population Survey (CPS) data (Besharov 1991), assuming that all children in families below the poverty line were eligible for Head Start and that only 5 percent of families above the poverty line were eligible. Our data were collected in fall 1989 and winter-spring 1990 (a time period apparently comparable to the 1990 fiscal year of the Administration on Children, Youth, and Families (ACYF). The ACYF estimated enrollments of 540,000 children in Head Start in 1990; the National Child Care Survey (NCCS) estimate was 583,734. Our estimate of the proportion of poor 4-year-old children enrolled in Head Start (29 percent) was lower than that obtained for 1989 from CPS data (34.2 percent) and was much lower than the estimate for 1990 (40.6 percent). However, it was within the large confidence interval (plus or minus 13 percentage points), due to small sample sizes.

We identified several possible reasons for the discrepancy:

- Parental misreporting of their child's Head Start status. High-income parents may report their child as being enrolled in Head Start when he or she is in a related or co-located program.

- The NCCS and CPS use household income in their calculation of poverty status. However, the Head Start program may use the family unit as the unit for eligibility. Thus a subfamily (e.g., teenage parent living with her mother) may be eligible, whereas counting the income of the teen's entire household would put the household considerably above the poverty line.

- Although the NCCS correctly reproduces the overall incomes of households in the United States, it does

FIGURE D.1

Enrollments in Head Start for All 3–5-Year-Olds by Poverty Status and Age of Child

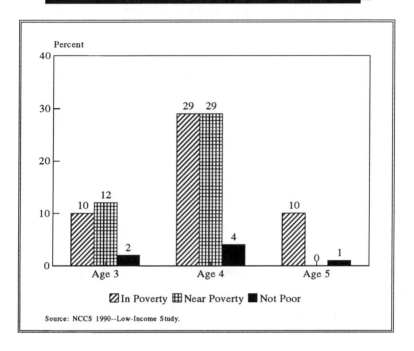

Source: NCCS 1990--Low-Income Study.

not correctly reproduce the incomes of children. The NCCS estimate of the proportion of children in poverty (500,000) is smaller than that found by others using the CPS (800,000). Consequently, the NCCS may be underestimating the proportion of poor children.

- Parents may be inaccurately reporting their incomes to Head Start grantees who determine program eligibility. They may report only their own incomes and not that of others in the family, or they may falsely claim that they do not work, and so on.

- Finally, we know that eligibility is determined only once, and that family incomes change over time. Consequently, some of those once eligible may no longer be, especially those interviewed in the spring or in their second year of Head Start.

Improvements in Data Quality

To improve the quality of the data, Urban Institute staff did the following:

- They examined the sample of Head Start families to see whether some of the nonpoor families contained subfamilies that may be eligible.

- They compared Head Start enrollment rates in poor families with and without subfamilies.

- They reweighted the sample to accurately represent the distribution of children in poverty, to see what effect this would have on the enrollment figures. Reweighting the number of children to bring the totals up to the CPS estimates of poverty produced an estimate of 792,437 children below the poverty line. That figure is close to the 800,000 4-year-olds that were estimated from the CPS for 1989 and 1990. However, the NCCS still reports 134,769 4-year-olds in families above the poverty line enrolled in Head Start. The total enrollment of poor 4-year-olds in Head Start (32 percent), based on the reweighted NCCS numbers, is slightly higher than the proportion obtained using the original weights (29 percent), and brings us much closer to the number obtained from the CPS for 1989 of 34.2 percent, although still below the 40.6 percent estimated for 1990.

We also found that some of the discrepancy can be explained by the difference between household and family income. Including only those families that do not have a secondary family in the same household increases the proportion of poor 4-year-old children enrolled in Head Start from 32 percent to 34 percent. We now have reproduced the CPS enrollment rate of 34 percent for 1989, still lower than the 40.6 percent estimated enrollment rate for 1990.

The reader should note that the data in the present report have not been reweighted to adjust for underrepresentation of poor children. Although reweighting the sample increases the size of the poor population and increases Head Start enrollments by about 10 percent (a statistically insignificant amount), it still does not render the NCCS Head Start estimates exactly comparable to those obtained based on the CPS.

Implications for the Present Report

To the extent that poor children are underrepresented in the NCCS and that their child care arrangements are more likely to be informal, we may be slightly overestimating the proportion of formal arrangements and underestimating the incidence of informal arrangements. Among the subsample of poor families, reweighting may change enrollments by a small but insignificant amount.

References

Besharov, Douglas J. 1991. *Child Care in the 1990s: Selected Statistics.* Washington, D.C.: American Enterprise Institute for Public Research.

Brush, Lorelei R. 1987. "Child Care Used by Working Women in the AFDC Population: An Analysis of the SIPP Data Base." Paper prepared for the Assistant Secretary for Planning and Evaluation of the U.S. Department of Health and Human Services by Analysis, Research and Training, McLean, Va. Photocopy.

Hofferth, Sandra L., April Brayfield, Sharon Deich, and Pamela Holcomb. 1991. *The National Child Care Survey, 1990.* Washington, D.C.: Urban Institute Press.

Sonenstein, Freya L. 1991. "The Child Care Preferences of Parents with Young Children: How Little Is Known." In *Parental Leave and Child Care: Setting a Research and Policy Agenda*, edited by J. S. Hyde and M. J. Essex, 337–53. Philadelphia: Temple University Press.

U.S. Bureau of the Census. 1989. *Statistical Abstract of the United States, 1989.* Washington, D.C.: U.S. Government Printing Office.